Can a Robot be Human?

Unputdownable ... a must-read book for anyone who is interested in philosophical problems and ideas.

Imre Leader, Professor of Mathematics,
Trinity College, Cambridge

Peter Cave's lively new book is full of interesting ideas, brow-creasing conundrums, persistent puzzles, and pleasing paradoxes. It is ideal reading for open and inquiring minds from 12 to 112—in fact for everybody who is just dipping a toe into philosophy for the first time. If it doesn't make you think, you are probably dead already.

Timothy Chappell, Professor of Philosophy,
The Open University

Entertaining, witty, and highly readable. A most enjoyable and illuminating read.

Michael Clark, Editor of Analysis *and Emeritus*
Professor of Philosophy, University of Nottingham

With skill and good humour, Peter Cave guides the reader through a maze of intriguing philosophical puzzles.

Lawrence Goldstein, Professor of Philosophy,
University of Kent

About the Author

Writer and broadcaster Peter Cave teaches philosophy for The Open University and City University, London. He chairs the Humanist Philosopher's Group and is often in debate, talking about paradoxes, while arguing for good reasoning, especially in ethical, political and religious life. He frequently contributes to philosophy magazines, from the serious to the fun, lectures abroad, and introduced BBC radio listeners to a paradoxical fair of fun.

Can a Robot
be Human?

33 Perplexing Philosophy Puzzles

Peter Cave

ONEWORLD
OXFORD

A Oneworld Book

Published by Oneworld Publications 2007
Copyright © Peter Cave 2007
Cover and text illustrations © Jolyon Troscianko 2007
Reprinted three times in 2007
Reprinted 2008

ISBN: 978–1–85168–531–8

Typeset by Jayvee, Trivandrum, India
Cover design by Mungo Designs
Printed and bound in Great Britain by CPI Cox and Wyman

Oneworld Publications
185 Banbury Road
Oxford OX2 7AR
England
www.oneworld-publications.com

Learn more about Oneworld. Join our mailing list to
find out about our latest titles and special offers at:
www.oneworld-publications.com

For Ardon Lyon

CONTENTS

CONTENTS

PREFACE

When I'm good, I'm very, very good; but when I'm bad,
I'm better.

Mae West

In these pages you will find philosophy – if you look. My recommendation is that you look first, rather than read this preface first. It is often better to taste than be told about tasting; better to love than be told about loving; and better to puzzle than be told about puzzling. So, I'll start this introduction again, for when (or if) you return to this page. I hope you will return, for here too there are puzzles.

In these pages you will find philosophy – if you look. My recommendation is that . . . I'd better not start all over again and engage in the endlessness which triggers certain unusual tales and puzzles; see, for example, *Therapy for tortoises* and *Just hanging around* (Chapters 5 and 11).

In these pages you *will* find philosophy; you will also find the puzzling, the paradoxical, the perplexing. You will find tales and tall stories, reasons and arguments, common sense and bizarre conclusions. While there are thirty-three chapters, there are, paradoxically, many more than thirty-three paradoxes or puzzles, taking us from saints and sinners, to the perils of love, to murders swathed with innocence, to the distress of a robot, to the metaphysics of time and to the myths of democracy.

Although the tone is largely light, some of the matters are deadly serious: sometimes literally, sometimes metaphorically. They are, indeed, matters that matter. Although their presentation is as paradoxes and puzzles, paradoxes and puzzles give rise to some of the deepest problems in philosophy: in metaphysics, logic and epistemology; in ethics, politics and aesthetics. Although the tales and reflections are, I hope, stimulating and sometimes amusing, they are not, I trust, 'dumbed down'. They make some challenging thoughts more readily accessible than they often are but they are not intended to suggest that the matters are not genuinely difficult, complex and unresolved.

I should like to think that this book is for everyone – for every woman, every man and every child – who is inclined to puzzle about the universe, about themselves and others and about how we should – and do – live and, yes, about grains of sand, bikini tops and sexual desire. I should like to think that this book appeals to people with no acquaintance with philosophy as well as to those with some and, indeed, to those with considerable acquaintance who may find it useful to be reminded of some puzzles for their next lecture series.

I should like to think those things but whether I should think them is another matter. That distinction, the distinction between what we should like to think and what we should think, is one at the heart of this book. The paradoxes, puzzles and per-plexities that follow show us that some of the things that we should like to think — that our reasoning, ethics and practices raise no questions — are not justified. Paradoxes, puzzles and perplexities remind us that there is a distinction — a further dis-tinction — between what appears to be so and what is really so.

'Food for thought' could aptly describe this work. Philosophy feeds those who want to muse, meditate and mull; it also feeds those who initially lack pleasure in such mental activities but who, once exposed to the subject's bafflements, acquire a taste for it that rarely goes away. The philosopher's cuisine is generous. Here is a *smorgasbord* (I've always wanted to write that) of paradoxes, puzzles and perplexities concerning the nature of time and space, of free will and determinism, of the self (what am I?) and of what morality demands.

Paradoxes, puzzles, perplexities – and Monty Hall

A witty quip, such as the one from Mae West that heads this preface, can momentarily puzzle because it seems to involve contradiction. But then revelation occurs, quelling the seeming – in this case, by our becoming aware of the alluded ambiguity of 'good' and 'bad'; well, good and bad at what?

Philosophical problems can often be cast as paradoxes, puzzles or perplexities which fascinate through generating apparent contradictions. We strive for revelation; we seek for the ambiguity, the false presupposition, the mistake in reasoning, to ease our unease. Yet the answers continue to leave many dissatisfied, either because they are unconvinced by some steps or because the answers raise new perplexities. The contradictions are often deeply rooted in our lives or language; 'surely, something has gone wrong', for we resist the thought that the world could itself be contradictory: how could it be? A contradiction can be readily produced in the sense of writing it down or saying it. I could easily say, 'This page contains a million words and it does not contain a million words.' But what I said could not possibly describe how things are or could be. What sense can be made of the thought that one and the same city, Athens, is both capital of Greece and not capital of Greece? How can the world be such a place that space is divisible, yet not divisible? What grasp can be made of our having free will, yet everything we do also being determined by events not under our will?

Some philosophers use the term 'paradox' very narrowly, very formally, concerning just those apparent contradictions that derive directly from our grasp of the nature of truth, of meaning or of mathematics. I – and many others – use the term far more widely, employing 'paradoxes', 'puzzles' and 'perplexities' more or less interchangeably. In this sense, a paradox arises when there is a clash in our beliefs, a clash that we cannot readily resolve, for the beliefs are either highly plausible or derive from other highly plausible beliefs, as, I hope, the following pages bring out.

A paradox involves a piece of reasoning, a piece of reasoning that strikes us as excellent. The reasoning starts with some premisses – beliefs, propositions or principles – which seem obviously true. When we reason from true premisses – and our reasoning does not go wrong – we reach true conclusions. A paradox, however, has a conclusion that, in some way, hits us as manifestly false, unacceptable or undesirable – a conclusion that contradicts what we take to be obviously true. What has gone wrong? Can we spot errors within the reasoning or are there underlying assumptions that merit rejection? May one or more of the premisses – which appear so blatantly true – not be true? Or perhaps we need to embrace the conclusion that seems so obviously false? Something has to give.

Something has to give because, although we may casually speak of this being a contradictory world, we cannot, as already mentioned, make sense of the world really being contradictory. We cannot make sense of its being the case that you are both reading these words and not reading these words at the same time. On the one hand, you may be doing something else as well as reading these words and, on the other hand, you may be doing something less than reading; skimming but not paying attention, and so on. But you cannot both be reading and not reading at the same time.

All these puzzles continue to keep philosophers in business, arguing over what are the right answers. All reveal long-standing philosophical problems. Many are traditional but I've given a fair number a new look. I have deliberately ignored examples, often to do with probability, that typically strike people as reaching surprising conclusions yet over which there is no serious dispute about the reasoning and no serious dispute about which answers are right. Perhaps I should add a caveat to that disregard of mine; for let me offer one example: the Monty Hall Show.

In the Monty Hall Show, there are three doors, A, B and C. One door has a desirable prize behind it. The other two doors each have a goat behind them. (For this puzzle we assume that goats are neither desirable nor desired but we are perhaps being speciesist; see Chapter 17 *Girl, cage, chimp*.) You want the prize and you can play a sequence of games. Which door hides the prize is chosen at random. Consider a game. You choose a door: say A. Perhaps you choose it in each game; that is irrelevant. Maybe a goat lurks behind door A; maybe the prize. You do not yet know. Your chosen door remains closed but the show's commère or presenter – and she knows what is behind each door – opens one of the other doors, B or C, to show you where one of the goats sits. (There is bound to be at least one goat that she can display, for even if there is a goat behind your chosen door A, there must be another behind either B or C.) Let us say that she opens B, displaying a goat. She then asks you if you want to change your choice from door A to B or C.

Obviously, you do not want to change to B (for that hides a goat) but you could change from A to C. You do not know whether the prize is behind A or C. All that you have discovered is that B is definitely ruled out. The puzzle is: is it rational to change your mind? That is, would you increase your chances of winning, over a sequence of games, if you changed your mind each time?

The solution, a solution over which thoughtful philosophers and mathematicians are agreed, is provided in 'Notes, sources and references' at the end of this book. In contrast to Monty Hall, the other problems in this book continue to give rise to perplexities – usually significant perplexities – in philosophy and for philosophers.

I have sought, in the main, to provide big and famous puzzles, with allusions to many others. I have also provided steers towards possible solutions – or, better, dissolutions – of the problems. Many great minds, over many centuries, have battled with the underlying problems; many great minds, over many centuries, have given conflicting answers. You may rightly reason that this author, therefore, is unlikely to be giving many (if any) definitive answers – and certainly I make no pretence to 'the' answers. In the pages that follow there are suggested approaches to resolution.

Wittgenstein considered giving his major work, *Philosophical Investigations*, a Shakespearean motto, 'I teach you differences.' In a short introductory work, there is the danger of not sufficiently heeding that teaching – the danger of letting fine distinctions, caveats and qualifications fall by the wayside. It is useful, when reflecting on the paradoxes, to look out for conflations, slidings and sleights of hand. None, I hasten to add, has been wittingly included. Although the book possesses its fair share of 'may's, 'maybe's and 'perhaps's, there is perhaps (!) value in quoting John Maynard Keynes who writes, '. . . the author must, if he is to put his point of view clearly, pretend sometimes to a little more conviction than he feels.'

Using this book

It was once commonly said that an apple a day keeps the doctor away. Who knows what the current, and no doubt transient, health advice is? Let us have some non-transient health advice for our minds. Here we have a puzzle a day, with two or three to spare, for a calendar month, or a puzzle a week for a good half-year. Each puzzle stands alone; there is no preferred order for reading them. If this book has any value, it is in its readers dipping in and pondering on the perplexities raised.

Let a paradox linger in your mind. If you prefer metaphorical flights of fancy, consider a paradox as an unusual wine or beer: swirl it around within your mouth, take in the flavour, sense new nuances of scent. You may find yourself enjoying the drink, uncovering more hidden temptations as you sip on. Enjoy, too, the intoxication of these wine-dark puzzles, but beware of intoxications interfering with reasoning.

If you have a strong dislike for such metaphorical flowers and flavours, forget the wine and beer — just think hard about the paradox and where it leads. Take it with you on your way to work, play or sleep; muse upon it with colleagues, friends or lovers; ponder upon it in the bar, bath or bed. Spread the paradoxes around. Philosophy is contagious and, in this instance, contagion is for the good.

Socrates went overboard, perhaps, when he told us that the unexamined life is not worth living; sometimes we feel that it is best not to examine some aspects of life. Certainly, for most people, there is value in reflecting on the universe and our place within. Aristotle commented that philosophy begins with curiosity and wonder. I hope that these puzzles will set you a-wondering and becoming more curious; hence I have provided quite a few detailed notes and references together with some, more general, further reading.

ACKNOWLEDGEMENTS

I have benefited from discussions with students and colleagues over many years at The Open University and City University, London, though the latter institution has sadly, mistakenly — and radically – reduced the philosophy available. Of great value have been the meetings of the Aristotelian Society, the Royal Institute of Philosophy and the University of London's Institute of Philosophy, most meetings of which are free and open to the public. This needs to be more widely known.

I should like to thank various editors for the stimulus to produce papers in accessible form, notably those of *Philosophy Now*, *Think* and *The Philosophers Magazine* and also Julian Mayers and Nick Romero for witty BBC broadcasting encouragements that fired up paradoxical thinking. Special thanks, for such encouragement, go to Rick Lewis, editor of *Philosophy Now*. A few of my approaches here have featured in those papers. I also thank Jurģis Šķilters and Valetin Muresan, of the

Universities of Latvia and Bucharest respectively, for their invitations to give puzzling talks and for their hospitality.

Turning to philosophical cuts and thrusts – and sometimes more – my thanks go to Michael Clark, Jerry Valberg, Ossie Hanfling (now sadly deceased), Arnold Zuboff, Martin Holt, Pippa Allison, Seth Crook, John Shand and the Humanist Philosophers' Group; and to Johanna Degenhardt and Tamsin Hoyle for literary suggestions, Donika Cheng on practical matters and Jolyon Troscianko for some happy illustrations. I thank Martha Jay and her Oneworld colleagues for encouraging me to write this book and for suffering my little yens. Regarding many aiding areas, a special gratitude goes to Angela Joy Harvey. Laurence Goldstein deserves particular commendation for initiating many paradoxical discussions over the years and for providing much philosophical stimulus, humour and, yes, erudition.

My greatest philosophical debt is to Ardon Lyon. I have learned most from this fine philosopher and friend who, even as I write, still foolishly has many books only 'out of print'. He has suffered much, having read all these puzzles at some developmental stage. He has made numerous helpful comments, with good humour, insight, even truth, as well as providing occasional apples and butler services and loud laughs. It is to Ardon Lyon that I dedicate this book.

There are certain to be mistakes in the body of this book. This has been thought to generate the paradox of the preface. Surely I believe what I have written and what I believe, I believe to be true. By asserting that there are some mistakes, I seem to commit myself wittingly to believing some falsehood or other. Were there no mistakes in the body of the book, then I am believing a falsehood in believing that there are; and if there are mistakes, then some claims that I make in the book I believe to be false. The tale grows more complicated, if we count this preface as part of the book's body.

Maybe I could avoid paradox by modifying the paragraph above (or the whole book), by introducing it with the words 'I assert that . . .' To see how this could (allegedly) effect nimble paradoxical escape, see Chapter 14's end. In recognition, however, of Ardon's being a true friend, philosopher and also philosophical, let me add that, as he has read all the chapters (true, only in early stages), he is responsible for any remaining errors. His shoulders are as broad as his laugh is loud.

Peter Cave

1

THE DANGERS OF HEALTH

You are a surgeon – and a bit of a philosopher. You are the head of a first-class team of organ transplant specialists that has an immaculate record of successful results. On your waiting list are four young people, all desperately ill and urgently in need of transplants without which they will soon die. Andrea requires a liver transplant, Barry a heart, Clarissa a pancreas and Donald a set of lungs. No donors are available. You are in despair. You did not enter medicine for money; you wanted to help people and improve their lives, yet here you are, watching four people die. These people have done nothing wrong; they would have long and happy lives ahead, but for their illnesses. If only organs were available, all would be well – for you have overcome the problems of tissue matching, rejection and so on.

As you are about to tell your patients there is no hope, you note the arrival of the new receptionist – a young man, namely, Eric. You know from his medical records that he is healthy. Your

eyes light up. You ask Eric to accompany you into the operating theatre, to show him around, of course, of course . . . Your quiet reasoning is:

> I want to do my best for as many people as possible. By killing Eric, I am in a position to distribute his organs to Andrea, Barry, Clarissa and Donald, saving their lives. True, the world no longer has Eric; that is, indeed, a sad loss. But the world has gained the other four lives. Four for the price of one is an excellent deal.

Of course, killing Eric would currently be illegal but our aim is what is morally the right thing to do. If we do nothing, we lose Andrea and the others, but Eric lives on. If we sacrifice Eric, we lose his life, but gain four. Assuming that in terms of quality of life – relationships with family, contributions to society – all the individuals are similar, the moral question would seem to rest solely on quantity, on the number of lives saved. Yet, curiously, many people are horrified at the thought of killing one innocent individual, even to save a greater number.

Morally, ought you not to kill one person to save the lives of others?

Most of us are pretty inconsistent in our views on the importance of *life*. (Let us assume, by the way, that we are here speaking solely of human life.) In war, many people readily accept that innocent civilian lives will be destroyed to secure the greater safety of others. Or, bringing the concern closer to home, many people will die sooner than they otherwise would because governments, instead of increasing spending on health care, keep taxpayers happy with low taxes. Further, some of the money raised through taxation is spent on the arts, prestigious sports projects and government entertainments. Were this money not so spent, it could be used to improve care for the elderly and poor, reducing the numbers that die each year. Our current society is such that many lives are lost merely to ensure a better quality of life for others.

However, you, the surgeon, are proposing to kill Eric to *save* four lives, not merely to increase their quality. Hence, ought we not to support your reasoning? If we think that we should, we may be following, somewhat crudely, the moral doctrine known as 'utilitarianism', in which the right action is that which will (or is likely to) bring about the greatest happiness of the greatest number. Is that what we should seek? Most people would say 'no' to the idea. 'No one has a right to use my organs against my will,' they insist.

*　　　*　　　*

Many announce that we simply have rights over ourselves — self-ownership — and that it is morally wrong for anyone, against our consent, to invade us, take our organs or kill us, unless we have ourselves done wrong. Some push this further, arguing that we also have rights over our labour and the results of our labour; hence, most taxation is a form of theft. Such rights form the bedrock of morality and such a morality makes the individual king. That is the idea.

If the individual is king, it is morally wrong to bring about an innocent individual's death as the means to something else, however worthy, such as saving the lives of four others. Eric's death, though, *is* required for the others to live. Of course, sometimes killings happen as a result of doing what is morally right, yet they are unintended, even if foreseen. The killing of innocent civilians is not usually an aim of war; rather it is (or is said to be) a very unfortunate side effect. Such unintended killing of civilians is justified in a just war, it is often argued, and is morally different from the killing of civilians that is the intended aim of some terrorists.

In contrast to making the individual king and drawing a distinction between intended outcomes and foreseen side-effects, the utilitarian ideal of the greatest happiness of the greatest number simply puts the top priority on what is the overall outcome regarding happiness. Whether deaths are side-effects or deliberate intentions, if the outcomes are the same, then, for the utilitarian, there is no morally relevant difference. For the utilitarian, there is no moral distinction between, for example, acts of war and acts of terrorism, *if* the consequences are the same.

Even if we adopt the utilitarian stance, we may fault the surgeon's argument. Healthy individuals would feel highly insecure (as they do from indiscriminate terrorist acts), if there were a policy of kidnapping and killing them to use their organs. Remember, those who benefit from the treatment may themselves become victims. Because of this insecurity, total happiness may well decrease in a society with such surgeons. Of course, this is so only if people know the policy is in operation. Suppose it became a secret government policy? Well, this is where too much utilitarian reasoning may damage our health.

Looking healthy? Perhaps 'tis best to avoid walking too near a transplant hospital.

6. IN THE BEGINNING

17. GIRL, CAGE, CHIMP

2

FICTIONAL FEELINGS?

It was astonishing. A large number of people looked on intently as a woman was manhandled by a group of ruffians, beaten, raped and left for dead. The gang had already killed her husband. No one intervened, though the crowd was well aware of everything that was happening, happening before their very eyes. It was macabre. And they ended up hooting and clapping. Not one of them called the police.

Is this the opening statement by the prosecution at a murder trial? Were the onlookers accomplices or just scared of the attackers? In the cold light of subsequent days, were they ashamed of their behaviour, of their cowardice, of doing nothing to help the victims?

The answer to all these questions is the same: 'Not at all.' The onlookers were in a theatre, watching a play. They knew it to be a work of fiction, yet – paradoxically – most were highly involved with the characters. They worried about what would happen to the woman; some felt shivers when the gang leader made his threats, his knife's blade gleaming. They pitied some characters, felt proud of others and hoped justice would eventually be done. Some were on the verge of weeping. As they left the theatre, they discussed how much they felt for the woman. A few awoke in the night, wondering how the characters' lives would develop; a few wondered how things might have gone differently.

We are moved by fictional characters, whether they appear in television soap operas, detective stories or popular films, or are famous individuals from the classics – Romeo and Juliet, Lolita or Lady Macbeth – in productions by the Royal Shakespeare Company, the National Theatre or the Royal Opera House. Typically, viewers and readers are fully aware that the characters are but fictions, yet the fictions may appear as alive as real people – and not just at the times of performance. Some viewers of soap sagas wonder what the fictional characters are doing between episodes. Is not this very odd, contrasting with, for example, wondering what is happening to celebrities answering to weird demands in reality television programmes?

Why do we feel emotions – love, hate, fear, regret, admiration – towards fictional individuals?

When we feel emotions – being scared by Dracula, pitying the young Jane Eyre or feeling angry at Bill Sykes' treatment of Nancy in *Oliver Twist* – we must surely believe, or at least half believe, that the individuals exist and possess features that justify our fear, pity or anger. We know that fictional entities are indeed fictional and lack existence; yet, paradoxically, we experience emotions towards them – or so it seems.

If we stress the sincerity of the audience's belief in, and feeling of emotion towards, what is being represented on stage or in writing, we should expect the audience to be up there, entering into the action in some way. Stress the audience's knowledge that it is just a play, a book, an opera and we are baffled by the audience's being moved – indeed, moved sometimes even to tears.

Irrationality is one answer. Certainly, we can believe and engage in many irrational things. Our emotions too can result from irrationality or mistaken beliefs but the emotions usually fade when we realize our mistakes. Members of mobs that shout death threats outside paediatricians' homes undergo (one hopes) emotional change when they discover paediatricians differ from paedophiles. Even if paedophiles have correctly been spotted, the anger and hatred may (again one hopes) be reduced by reflection on better ways to help. When we are scared of spiders we think poisonous, our fears should be quelled once we are convinced that the spiders are harmlessly living non-poisonous lives. In some cases, however, although we know such truths, our fears irrationally persist. And so can our emotions, even when we know the objects of those emotions to be but fictions.

Irrationality may yet prove to be too easy an answer or, on reflection, not an easy answer at all, if intended to carry conviction. The most rational of people can be moved by fictions yet, even when moved, know full well that they are seated in a theatre, reading a book or watching television. Or do they? Perhaps, one way or another, they suspend their belief in the stagy surroundings, suspend their memories of the tickets they purchased or block out the sound of the book's rustling pages. Perhaps they fall for what is represented as being real, as being, indeed, all for real. Remember though, they cannot be taken in that much: if they were, they would be warning of danger, calling a doctor or exposing the villain – as children sometimes do when at pantomimes.

If irrationality is no right answer, perhaps the emotions are not directed at the fictional characters at all. It has been suggested that fiction leads the audience to have the fear, the pity, the joy – and so on – at real people (not the fictions) who have the relevant characteristics. The causes of emotions need not be the objects at which the emotions are directed. You feared your neighbour's hound (or so you thought) but what caused that fear might have been no hound but a radio's blaring. It is the radio's sound – sound that you *mistook* as canine threatening howls – that caused your fear. Returning to fictions, the pity that comes from reading Charles Dickens' portrayal of the poor, for example, is not directed at the novel's characters but at those in poverty, in the real, real world. The tale brings those real people to mind.

Although this approach to the fictional puzzle makes sense, it lacks plausibility. Often, do we not feel approval for, pity towards or are angered by the fictional characters? Why think we are mistaken? Furthermore, perhaps the approach requires us to have specific real individuals in mind to account for our emotions, yet we rarely have such real individuals in mind when watching a play.

Other attempted solutions to puzzling fictions have rested on claiming that our emotions towards fictional characters are make-believe emotions. Such solutions also lack conviction. The tears we experience when moved by some fictions are real enough; maybe the pity is too.

*   *   *

The very thought of things can generate emotions, without the need for full belief or disbelief – and perhaps that is enough for handling this puzzle. We do not really *believe* that the woman is being harmed, as we watch the staged action; perhaps the mere *thought* (or some other distinct psychological state) of her being harmed is enough to generate our pity, disgust or whatever. Our thoughts are carried along by the play, book or opera and generate real emotions. Whether or not this is the right approach, we should not lapse into arguing that we are therefore directing our emotions at mere thoughts or ideas. Romeo and Juliet fall in love and die tragically and their tragic love brings tears to our eyes. An idea or thought of Romeo and Juliet cannot itself fall in love. Our thoughts and ideas are *of* Romeo and Juliet, *of* Lolita, *of* the latest arrivals in a soap saga such as *EastEnders* or comedies such as *Seinfeld* and *Fawlty Towers*. Quite what constitutes the relationship between us and non-existent entities, such as fictions, remains obscure. Obscurities may multiply, if we reflect on the peculiar attraction of opera; we may be moved by a character's plight, while simultaneously and incongruously applauding the soprano's vocal skills.

The paradox of fiction has spin-offs. Curiously, we can experience suspense, even when we know what is coming. Many people have seen Alfred Hitchcock's 1960 film, *Psycho*, more than once. The shower scene, with the throbbing music, can still cause suspense even after repeated viewings. The pulse quickens and tingles run down the back – despite our knowing the unhappy and blood-stained outcome, a bloody outcome paradoxically rendered in black and white.

Suspense is just one example of the unpleasant emotions that, it seems, we go out of our way to encounter in novels, film and music. Tragedies cause pain; horror stories cause fear – but we enjoy them. Why? What is going on?

Aristotle suggested that such experiences of fiction provide us with emotional release – catharsis – that helps us carry on in life. Quite how and why this should work are questions that lack easy answers and which raise the further question of what, if anything, are the arts for? Or is that a fictional question?

33. IS THIS ALL THERE IS?

8. WILL YOU STILL LOVE ME TOMORROW?

30. EYE SPY

3

SYMPATHY FOR THE DEVIL

Once upon a time there was an all-powerful being – and nothing else. Following tradition, we use the pronoun 'he' for such a power. Religious believers would call him 'God', except he differed, in one vital respect, from the traditional God. True, he was all powerful and infinite; true, he was all knowing but, instead of being all good and benevolent, he was all bad and mean. Many may conclude that I have described a jumped-up version of God's fallen angel: the Devil. I shall speak of him as 'Devil' but, to reiterate, he is the *one* all-powerful being. There was no God to create him. He had no beginning.

Devil chose to create a universe, much like ours. It had stars and planets, of which at least one – Earth – had life just like our Earth. In all respects, Earth was the same as ours: it had oceans and mountains, people and nations. There was England, with warm beer, cricket and football; Scots cheering at English teams' frequent misses and losses. There were tigers, suitably striped, and tiger lilies too, alarms so alarming and so without point, mobile 'phones, designer clothes and techno music. There were petals, porcupines and cooing pigeons; safety regulations, sunbathing gazelles, wishing wells – English National Opera too – and so on and so forth.

There were people who argued about how the universe began. Religious texts existed – the Bible and Qur'an – as did churches and synagogues, temples and mosques; and people worshipped a great and glorious and all-good being, God: some even claimed divine revelations of his benevolence, his commands and his concern for each and every one, from sparrow to human.

Devil tried to laugh off this mistaken worship of an almighty good God. He had deliberately arranged for the scriptures to come about but as a joke. Deep down his devilish inside, it infuriated and upset him. Even the few devil-worshippers failed to recognize him, Devil, as the *one* almighty being.

What especially annoyed Devil was that theologians, philosophers and even lay people discussed the problem of evil, of suffering. How, given that there is an all-powerful and all-good God (as they mistakenly believed), could so much evil exist, in the form of suffering? Devil had reasoned that if he set the universe going, with so much pain and misery developing over the centuries, reflective people would conclude that there must be an all-powerful, all-bad creator, namely him, Devil. They should be discussing the problem of good. Given that there is so much evidence pointing to an all-powerful bad being – Devil – the puzzle should be why good exists.

Why believe there is an all-powerful, all-good God rather than an all-powerful, all-bad Devil?

Religious believers typically take the universe as evidence in favour of there being an all-good, all-powerful God. They sometimes argue that the world's particular features show that there must be a creator-designer who is, indeed, all good and powerful. Yet, as John Stuart Mill argued in the nineteenth century, if we seriously look around the world in order to work out, by analogy, what features an all-powerful creator must have, we find overwhelming evidence to blacken that creator's name. Millions of people have suffered, are suffering or will suffer disease or starvation, often dying painfully. These sufferings are accompanied by the misery of hopelessness and the misery of being unable to help each other, compelled impotently to look on. Millions of people have suffered war and torture. In more mundane, happier lives, vast numbers of people experience grief as friends and relatives die; vast numbers suffer distressing conditions at work – and so on. Billions of animals are racked with pain as other animals devour them, those other animals suffering when being devoured in turn. Small wonder Devil is upset when he hears 'Praise be to the loving God' and 'All things bright and beautiful'.

Whether we see the problem as that of the existence of good or that of the existence of evil, some have attempted solutions. We should bear in mind that an all-powerful anything – Devil or God – cannot do anything: he cannot bring about things which are contradictory or which, if he performed them, would be contradictory. Can an all-powerful being create an immoveable post? If he is all powerful, surely he can; but if he is all powerful, he can move it, so it is not immoveable after all. Being unable to do what it is logically impossible to do is not a constraint on power. If someone told you both completely to close this book and not to close it, at the same time, there is nothing that would count as doing it, so there is nothing there to be done and hence no constraint on what you can do.

Once we are aware that God or Devil cannot do what is logically impossible (for this consists of nothing at all actual or possible), we may argue that for there to be evil, there must, as a matter of logic, be good. Whatever the force of this point, it would never explain why there is *so much* good (or evil).

A popular move of godly believers is to speak of the value of free will. Free will makes the world a better place: it is better to have free agents than robots, better to have people freely choosing to perform good deeds than being predetermined or predestined to perform them. However, possessing free will means people can choose to inflict evil and they may make such a choice. Devil would, of course, argue in reverse. Free will gives considerable scope for lots of freely conducted evils, maliciousness and injustice – that is why he created free individuals. True, by having such creatures, Devil ran the risk that some would sometimes do good but that would be outweighed by the evil of people freely and intentionally causing suffering in the world.

The free will defence only works, if it works at all, in regard to goods and evils caused by people. There are puzzles about what free will is, but even assuming that we can make sense of it, there is no reason at all to believe that people have freely caused most earthquakes, volcanic eruptions, floods and diseases. Devil can rub his devilish metaphorical hands: such cruel disasters are evidence for his existence. Devil's problem is to explain why he created sources of happiness: blue skies and sunsets, oceans roaring, mountains soaring; the delights of love, the excitements of sex and the intoxications of music, wine and even philosophy. He may argue that, when things go wrong, these are effective ways of creating huge distress. And even when things go well, other people suffer through envy, jealousy and a sense of unfairness. Furthermore, for the lucky ones, there remains the awareness of the loss of such delights through infirmity and ultimately death. We may also draw attention to the despairing uncertainty for some over whether a good God exists. That is itself evidence for the maliciousness of Devil; after all, a good God would not tolerate such despair.

*   *   *

Many people believe that God exists. They often rely on scriptures and religious teachers but some look for evidence and believe it is found in certain features of the world around them. My suggestion of Devil is a way of challenging the inference from worldly features to an all-good God. Introducing Devil should also remind us that the choice is not simply between a God with benevolence and no God. Those who believe in an all-powerful figure that created and designed the universe need to explain why they are convinced he is all good rather than all bad – or, indeed, something in between. Is it not most likely that there are at least two distinct and powerful powers, one evil and one good? Zoroastrianism is typically taken as proclaiming such a duality. Is it the only sensible religion? Paradoxically, that could explain why hardly anyone believes in it. Mind you, maybe that is no paradox at all. After all, do faith and good sense readily combine?

These days Devil is left out of the options and out in the cold. Small wonder he is distressed; no wonder he merits our sympathy. The sympathy, though, could be more aptly applied to both Devil and God, to both gods and devils, not because they lack recognition but, paradoxically, because they lack existence – or is that one paradox – and an atheistic leap – too far?

22. A BIT RICH

10. MARY, MARY, QUITE CONTRARY

21. SAINTS, SINNERS AND SUICIDE BOMBERS

32. MYSTERIES

4

HE WOULD SAY THAT, WOULDN'T HE?

A politician, a government minister indeed, has been caught, literally and metaphorically, with his trousers down. Let's call him 'Sir Cedric'. Sir Cedric is fighting for his political career. Through the media, he abjectly apologizes:

> True, I've been unfaithful to my wife. I've lied and cheated to go off with a floosie or two – or three or more. All that, I now deeply, deeply regret. But, trust me, although I have deceived in matters of love, of romance and sex, I am utterly and completely honest in my political ways, in my sincerity in doing what is best for the country and, for that matter, in everything else. True, I cannot be trusted over affairs of the heart but I am a man of integrity when it comes to affairs of the State.

The matter is of public concern: if public representatives lie to their spouses, are they likely to lie to the electorate? Is it rational to believe Sir Cedric? He has owned up to lying sometimes, so he may be lying now. Perhaps he deceives people not only about affairs of the heart but also about affairs of State. Of course, he may be telling the truth: perhaps he is, as he says, a man of honour in his public service. He succumbs to deceit only when driven by passions of the flesh. However, now we know that at least one thing has a higher priority for him than telling the truth (one that can interrupt his truth telling), maybe there are other things. Sir Cedric's declaration is an instance of the announcement: 'I am prepared to mislead you over matters concerning such-and-such but *only* over such matters, not over anything else.'

Although such a speaker may well be speaking the truth, do we have any good reason to believe him, now we know truth telling is not his highest priority in some announcements? If he is telling the truth about his deceit, clearly he lies on some occasions. If he is not speaking the truth, then he is lying right now. Either way, he undermines his commitment to truth telling. A politician intent on, for example, financial fraud as well as romantic fraud, but exposed only in the romantic, may well make the same claim as Sir Cedric makes.

In the trial concerning the Profumo sex scandal, Lord Astor denied that he had slept with Miss Mandy Rice-Davies. She famously commented, 'He would say that, wouldn't he?' Paradoxically, when speakers (unlike Lord Astor) are open and tell the truth in specifying limitations on their truth telling, they also expose themselves to the Rice-Davies riposte.

Is it rational to trust people at all, if they tell us that in some matters they deceive?

I derive this little puzzle from Machiavelli. Machiavelli, in early sixteenth-century Florence, recommends that politicians should deceive the public when it helps to promote the common welfare – but only then. If we think of Machiavelli as a politician, what are we to make of what he tells politicians to do? Maybe he is deceiving them in what he says? Maybe he seeks to deceive far more extensively but does not want to own up?

We often do compartmentalize our lives; we often do know that people are more likely to mislead over some matters than others – perhaps in affairs of the heart but not affairs of State. People who are completely honest in their dealings with friends sometimes lie in wage negotiations about the final offers they would accept. People who would not dream of cheating their newsagent may delight in financial windfalls that arrive courtesy of accounting mistakes by banks and large department stores. This knowledge of how people deceive in one area and not another cannot derive solely from what they tell us. Rather, experience shows us that some people can be trusted in some spheres but not others. Indeed, we may well use our own predilections as a guide to those of others.

*   *   *

Utilitarianism tells us to maximize happiness. That aim, some would argue, takes priority over telling the truth: it trumps truth telling. We should tell the truth only if it is likely to secure more happiness than would deception. Sometimes deception needs to be deployed because sometimes that will maximize happiness; think of little white lies. We know, then, that individuals who wittingly announce that they are utilitarians of this ilk are prepared to deceive. If their announcement is true, they explicitly own up to being prepared to deceive; if their announcement is false, clearly they sometimes deceive. Given their deceptive propensities, if we rely solely on their statements, then, paradoxically, we are at sea over whether, in telling us they are utilitarian, they are even telling us the truth that they are utilitarian. And when they tell us that utilitarianism is the correct morality to adopt, again, we flounder.

The default position is to believe what people tell us – yet if people truthfully tell us of the limits of their truth telling, we cannot rationally rest our belief in what they say on what they say. What they say is akin to saying 'I may be misleading you in what I am saying.' This does not possess the contradiction of the liar who says 'I am lying' (see Chapter 31), but it should undermine its hearers' beliefs in what is being said. Paradoxically, people's truthful comments about their limits on truth telling are 'doubt generators', as I term them.

Reassuring hearers that we are speaking the truth creates its own absurdity. If our hearers already distrust us, why should they believe us when we say we are telling the truth? If they already believe us truthful, we fail to *inform* them in telling them of our veracity. If anything, our attempt to tell people of our truth-telling ways may itself be a doubt generator, raising suspicions about our commitment to truth.

Trust me, I am telling you the truth.

14. DON'T TELL HIM, PIKE!

31. DON'T READ THIS NOTICE

 1. THE DANGERS OF HEALTH

5

THERAPY FOR TORTOISES

Allow me to introduce you to Mr T., a wealthy tortoise from lands of Ancient Greece. Speak forth, Mr T. Explain how you became so wealthy.

'Being but a humble tortoise, I was always laughed at for my slowness of gait. When I tried to run, the laughter turned to ridicule, sometimes even crude mockery. Other creatures sped by me, waving, cackling, calling me "Speedy Gonzales". I was downtrodden; I felt truly rotten and rubbish. But then, my life changed. I discovered Professor Zeno of Elea: "Zany", to his friends.'

Would you explain yourself, Mr T.?

'Zany (well, I called him "Professor" at the time, of course) set up a mile-long race between Mr Achilles and me. Mr Achilles was the fastest runner in Athens. At first, I thought the Professor was intent on making a fool of me – pulling my leg or tap-dancing on my shell. But that was not so. You see, I was given one hundred yards' start. That was only fair, as Mr Achilles ran much more quickly than I did. Let's say, twice as fast.'

But how did the hundred yards' start help? Presumably Achilles still won the race.

'That's what everyone predicted. I got amazing odds when having, as I thought, a mad moment and putting my faith in the Prof., I placed some large bets on Mr Achilles never catching me.'

What happened?

'The starting gun was fired. But before Achilles could win the race, he had to overtake me, you see. And before he could overtake me, he had to get level with me.'

True enough — but that was just a hundred yards.

'Achilles raced forward to the point where I had been. By the time he'd completed that hundred yards, I had moved fifty yards further, running at half his speed.'

So, he had just those fifty yards to run to catch up.

'Indeed. But by the time he ran those fifty, I had gone another twenty-five.'

Well, so then he ran those extra twenty-five.

'Quite so. But by the time he'd done that, I'd gone twelve and a half further.'

Yes, yes — but the distances for him to run are getting smaller and smaller.

'Don't you see? Achilles could never catch me, let alone overtake me. Whenever he got to where I'd been, I'd moved a little further. Half, then quarter, then one eighth, then one

sixteenth of that initial hundred yards' start. That's an infinite series. Those proportions, though ever-decreasing, go on endlessly . . . Endlessly . . . Endlessly . . .'

Ah, so that accounts for your wealth, Mr T.? Presumably, you collected your winnings?

'Indeed I did sir – and in cash – all thanks to Zany Zeno. He's brought me right out of my shell.'

How can we ever manage to move at all?

Zany, I mean, Zeno, gave us four famous paradoxes of motion, in support of his teacher, Parmenides, who argued that all motion and change are illusory. To reach Mr T., Achilles needed to complete the endless series of half, then quarter, then eighth and so on. For you to walk to the wall opposite, you must go half the way, then half of the half, then half of that half: again, an endless series. Of course, Mr T. has the same problem. He keeps tortoisely quiet about that, slipping back into his shell. How can he move to a place or even slip back into his shell? How can an endless series ever be completed? Yet complete such series, it seems that we must, whenever we move.

Mathematicians often think they have the puzzle solved. They tell us that many series, for example the one just mentioned, are indeed infinite, yet partial sums of the series converge within a limit. The series of half plus a quarter plus an eighth plus . . . – take the series as far as you like – well, whichever ones you take, they can be shown to converge towards one. Achilles ran one hundred yards, then half of one hundred, then half of that half and so on; hence, at the two hundred yard point, he drew level with Mr T. Similarly, the times taken to run those distances became progressively shorter, the partial totals also converging to a limit. The reducing size of the spatial distances was matched by the reducing size of the temporal durations.

Many philosophers are dissatisfied by this mathematical solution, for there remains the philosophical puzzle of how we can ever complete an *endless* number of runs or other movements, even if, indeed, the spans of time are also reducing in length. It is all very well to talk about mathematically converging to, or within, a limit, but that is no explanation at all of how in the physical world we reach the limit.

*   *   *

Movement is not at the heart of the paradox. Similar difficulties arise concerning anything extended, whether in space or in time. Consider an unmoving object, existing through any span of time. For it to have lasted for an hour, it must have completed an endless series of time spans: for example, half an hour, a quarter of an hour, an eighth, a sixteenth and so on. Or ignore time and consider an object extended in space, say one foot long: somehow that foot is made up of half a foot and a quarter and an eighth and a sixteenth – and so forth. There is also the puzzle of how anything can even get started in its existence through time or movement through space. Take any time span: the object must first have existed through half of that time span. Now consider that half time span: it must first have existed through half of that half and so on.

One thought is that we need to be careful about what we mean when we speak of endlessly dividing or dividing to infinity. Talk of infinity may wrongly lead us to think that infinity is a place we can reach; think of the queer claim that parallel lines meet at infinity. Just because we can conceive of any mentioned distance as being further divided, we must not leap to conclude that an infinity of divided distances actually exists.

Perhaps the direction towards a solution is to distinguish between abstract mathematical representations and what is represented. Consider a portion of any distance. The portion may be accurately represented by, for example, the fraction of one third – ⅓ – of the whole. That would seem to pose no problem. But it can also be represented by the endlessly recurring decimal number 0.333 . . ., causing our bewilderment about how that physical distance could contain an endless flow of distances diminishing by a tenth.

It is all very well for Mr T. to bathe in his wealth but if we cannot resolve the puzzles over the divisibility of space and time, all movement, all division, all separateness – all tortoises, all shimmering tortoise shells, all fluttering pages of paradox books – are but illusions. Indeed, all is one.

All is one?

9. SAND, SUN, SEA AND . . .

28. TENSIONS IN TENSE

6

IN THE BEGINNING

I am unfairly discriminated against.

Who am I? I am that person whom you failed to create some years ago, last year or maybe a few moments ago — that time when you avoided having sex or deployed contraception. There are billions and billions like me, all unfairly treated.

Those of you lucky enough to exist speak keenly about the value of human life. You make great efforts to keep people alive. You have legal systems, moral pressures, checks and balances designed to prevent people from being killed. You have hospitals, vaccinations and screening programmes; safety nets, health regulations, well woman and well man clinics, all to assist the living to carry on living. Virtually all of you are appalled by infanticide — at killing children, at killing babies. Most of you are repelled by very late abortions: what is the *morally relevant difference*, you say, between a new-born baby and a foetus in the womb a few hours before birth?

Some of you already treat abortion as morally equivalent to murder. If late abortions are akin to infanticide and hence are morally wrong, what of slightly earlier abortions – and earlier and earlier, as we count down the days? What is the morally relevant difference between a foetus of sixteen weeks and one that is a day younger – and what is the relevant difference between that foetus and one a little younger still? We may move on down the days in this way, going lower and lower, until we reach the moment of conception.

> Conception! That's what marks the difference. Before conception, there is no individual entity that is likely to grow into a person; there is no potential person present at all. It is only once the egg is fertilized that we have something that is potentially a person, with feelings, intelligence, loves and desires.

I charge you with being space-ist and number-ist. I would even say 'materialist' but for the fact that philosophers understand the term peculiarly. Yes, the egg and sperm, pre-conception, have some distance between them – their structure or matter is greatly spaced – but why is that numerical and geographical fact morally relevant? That there are two elements does not show that the twosome is not a potential person. True, we cannot tell beforehand which sperm will fertilize the egg towards which the sperms are heading – the egg which will grow into embryo, foetus, baby, child and adult. Undoubtedly, though, before fertilization, there must have existed the particular sperm – let's call him 'Herm' – which would end up fertilizing the particular egg – Eggwina. Were that not so, that fertilized egg would not have come about. Not to have engaged in uncontracepted sex at that moment (whenever it was) would have prevented Herm and Eggwina from uniting; it would have prevented creation of the fertilized egg and hence the foetus, baby and adult life that people so greatly value.

If it is wrong to kill people, isn't it also wrong not to create people?

To get to the nub of the question, let us move to babies. After all, there are simple replies to the question above. One would be that people usually do not want to die but people who are not yet created have no wants at all – well, not yet.

What is wrong with killing a baby? If the answer is simply in terms of the loss of its future life, a life which has value in itself, then abortion is also morally wrong. This is because had the abortion taken place, that future life (child, adult) would also have been lost. That future life would also have been lost had successful contraception been used, preventing the creation of the foetus which grew into the child who grew into the adult. Moving yet further back, sexual abstinence would have been wrong; it too would have prevented the existence of the child and later adult.

Being pregnant, of course, prevents the coming into existence of other foetuses. No one is arguing that it is possible to create all possible lives. Making more and more lives is also undesirable, if we are unable to support them. The puzzle is that if – *if* – what is wrong with infanticide and abortion is the loss of the future person who would otherwise come about, then contraception and, indeed, sexual abstinence, other things being equal, are similarly wrong. The chaste are as bad as the baby killers – at least with regard to the loss of the future lives that would otherwise exist. Yet most of us believe that to be a crazy conclusion. It is a conclusion that would paradoxically pop chaste monks and nuns, those committed to vows of chastity, next to murderers.

*   *   *

Arguably, the mistake is to think that what makes killing a human being wrong is the loss of that being's future life. A more plausible account is that what makes it wrong is the loss that the individual suffers. Consider Esmeralda, just a usual person (even if unusually named): she has a sense of her self continuing into the future. By killing her, we thwart her desires, her aims, her intentions. Fundamentally, Esmeralda wants to go on living. That is why it is wrong to kill her – and why it may well not be wrong to kill someone who really does want to die; why voluntary euthanasia and assisted suicide should be permitted. Further, if we have a being that lacks any sense of itself continuing into the future and so lacks any desire for that self to continue, then killing that individual painlessly cannot harm it. Of course, there may be other reasons, good reasons, why it is wrong to kill such individuals; we may, for example, cause distress to others.

In this approach, sexual abstinence, contraception and abortion are not wrongs to the individual who fails to develop.

This is because they involve no direct harm to a being that has a sense of self continuing into the future. No one seriously thinks the egg and the sperm have desires and intentions; no one seriously thinks the foetus does. For that matter, very young babies also lack such a sense of continuing self. Infanticide and some abortions, however, will still be wrong, in so far as they cause distress to others, notably and often the mother. And, human that we are, there may well be adverse knock-on effects, were we to allow our reason to diminish our natural discomfort or distress at very late abortions and infanticide.

For a response to the above general approach that seeks to justify us in not worrying about those whom we do not create, consider the principle, 'Do unto others as you would have them do unto you.' Most people are pleased to have been created (well, they tend to say that, though it could be self-deception). Were you to start creating children tonight, it is likely that the outcome would be people who are pleased that you did unto them what you are pleased was done unto you – namely, be created!

Does creating people count as doing something good to them? If so, you know your chat-up line for tonight – but beware, beware, the consequences.

17. GIRL, CAGE, CHIMP ➡️

9. SAND, SUN, SEA AND . . . ➡️

33. IS THIS ALL THERE IS? ➡️

7

THE INNOCENT MURDERER:
A NOBODY DUNIT

Three singers trek across the desert. Being modestly inclined, they have their own separate tents, facilities and provisions. Let us give our singing trekkers names: Lena, Poppy and Barrington. Desert life is no happy life and while Lena and Poppy get on well, singing duets as sopranos, they take a dislike towards Barrington's baritone tones. Lena and Poppy are unaware of how much the other dislikes baritone Barrington; they do not discuss such matters. Relations with Barrington deteriorate so much that the women, independently and unbeknownst to each other, decide they must kill him. Well, it is hot in the desert – and his singing *is* pretty bad.

One night, while Barrington is asleep, Poppy steals into his tent and pours poison into his water container. Poppy, the poisoner, returns to her tent. A little later, Lena, knowing nothing about Poppy's jaunt, tiptoes over to Barrington, finds his water

container and cracks the bottom, so that the water leaks out. Lena, the leaker, slips back to her tent. Early in the morning, before Barrington awakes, the women pack up their belongings and trek off, singing together, leaving Barrington alone. When Barrington awakes, he finds his water container empty; singing deeply and tragically, he dies of thirst. In due course, the desert police discover what has happened. The puzzle is: has either of the young ladies murdered Barrington?

Poppy argues: 'Yes, I wanted Barrington dead but I cannot be held guilty of murder. The poison didn't touch Barrington's lips. It had all drained away by the time he awoke. He didn't die of being poisoned.'

Lena argues: 'Yes, I too wanted Barrington dead and intended that he should die of thirst. In fact I drained away toxic water, so, if anything, I saved him from a horrible poisoning.'

Barrington is well and truly dead. It is difficult not to believe that Barrington has been murdered. Surely Poppy or Lena is a murderer? Yet are they not both innocent of murder? For Poppy to be a murderer, her actions should at least have caused Barrington's death, but she is right: she only poisoned the water and Barrington did not drink any poisoned water. For Lena to be a murderer, she should at least have caused Barrington's death, but Lena is right: she only drained out poisoned water, saving him from death by poisoning.

Can a murder be committed by the innocent?

Some will say that, as Barrington died of dehydration and Lena drained out the water, she is the murderer. But Lena drained out poisoned water and the poison could have been one that acted by causing dehydration, in which case it would perhaps not be quite so clear that Lena was the cause of death by dehydration – for Barrington would then have died that way in any case. Indeed, the poison might have made the water undrinkable or have solidified it, so Barrington would have died from dehydration, even without Lena's little leaking. Even were Lena clearly the cause of death, does that make her morally *the* murderer, given that, had she not acted, Barrington would have died courtesy of Poppy? Of course, it appears as if Lena did, unwittingly, prevent Poppy from murdering Barrington; she apparently did this by, unwittingly, making Poppy's poisoning ineffective. But appearances may be deceptive.

What is clearly missing in this *Desert Song* is a conspiracy. If the two women acted together as one, then maybe they could both be convicted of murder. Their actions, taken together, led to Barrington's death and that outcome was their intent. Acting separately, it seems that at best – or worst – they are each guilty of *attempted* murder but, arguably, innocent of murder.

An intention to do something wrong or against the law is rarely considered as bad as when the intention gets fulfilled. If we could be prosecuted solely for our intentions, however distant from success, we should almost all have criminal records. A comparison may be made with those religious doctrines which seem to collapse psychological states, including ones even more remote from actions than intentions, into the actions which could typically result. Following the New Testament, the former American president, Jimmy Carter, accepted that lusting in one's heart for a woman other than one's wife is morally the same as the act of adultery. More recently, some extreme feminists have bizarrely claimed that watching the portrayal of rape is the same as raping.

Lest this *Desert Song* seems far-fetched, consider the following, based on a real court case:

Phillips wanted a member of his gang, Daniels, dead. Indeed, he beat up Daniels, took him for dead and bundled him into the back of his car. Phillips decided he must get rid of the body, so he drove the car to the edge of a cliff and pushed it over. The police later discovered that the beating Phillips had dished out to Daniels failed to kill him; it merely knocked him unconscious. What killed Daniels was the downward journey from the cliff's edge to the rocks below. Was Phillips guilty of murder?

His defence counsel argued not. The argument went as follows. To murder people is intentionally to kill them. Phillips was guilty of attempted murder – witness the non-fatal beating that he gave Daniels, with the intention of killing him. However, what killed Daniels was the fall over the cliff's edge; but when Phillips pushed the car over the edge, he was not intending to kill Daniels but to dispose of the body. Phillips thought Daniels was already dead, so that action could not have been intended to kill him.

The judge failed to fall for the defence counsel's silver tongue. The judge ruled that the actions by Phillips should be taken as one and, taken as one, they or it resulted from Phillips' intention to kill and in Daniels' death.

*   *   *

These cases raise questions of the identity and individuation of actions. Actions are what we do; but quite what do we do? Last night, you woke the neighbours. Is that accurate? You turned up the music and the music woke the neighbours. Is that quite right? You twiddled a knob that caused the music level to rise that caused vibrations through the wall that woke the neighbours. Did you twiddle the knob – or did you, more accurately, move your fingers that caused the knob to turn? Where do we stop? Are there some 'basic' actions that we perform directly, that is, actions in which there are no further intermediate causal links? As well as the question of the identity of actions, we must contend with the identity of agents or subjects. Phillips is a single agent. In the killing of Barrington, Poppy and Lena were not, though when Poppy and Lena duet together, they sing as one.

Counting tables and chairs in the room is easy but when counting actions and agents, things sometimes fall apart – and sometimes come together.

24. LUCKY FOR SOME

25. 'I SHOT THE SHERIFF'

13. WOLVES, WHISTLES AND WOMEN

8
WILL YOU STILL LOVE ME TOMORROW?

And so the two swore that at every time of their lives, until
death took them, they would assuredly believe, feel and
desire exactly as they had believed, felt and desired during
the preceding weeks. What was as remarkable as the under-
taking itself was the fact that nobody seemed at all surprised
at what they swore.

Thomas Hardy, *Jude the Obscure*, 1895

There is something deeply puzzling about the commitments
that we make, into the distant future, when we know that
things will change.

Lovers, when in love, soar into sapphire skies, flying on
wild and wonderful wholehearted words of sincere commitment and devotion. 'We are meant for each other.' 'I cannot live
without you.' 'Our love will never die.' Literally understood,
these are false, yet lovers serve them to each other, intent on

conveying truths and, when seeking mutual assurances, they also play some startling questions: 'Will you love me, when I'm old and grey?' 'Do you want me just for my money?' 'Just because I'm sexy?' 'Would you love me were I paralysed, my mind gone, my character changed?'

These questions lead to a desperate plea. 'I want you to love me solely for myself, for being me, not for anything else, just for my true essence.' This is perilous metaphysics. What sense can we make of the *me*, the *self*, *my essence*, if it is meant still to exist, even when all other features of mine have changed?

What is it that we love, when we love someone?

Consider how we relate to items in the world. We want a drink but not just any drink will do. We definitely want a whisky – and whisky of a certain type, say, Talisker. At some stage, specifications cease. It matters not at all whether it is that or this particular glass of whisky – so long as the glass contains Talisker. This particular drink could be replaced by another; so long as it is of the same desired type, that is fine. Things are typically different with people with whom we have a special relationship. You want to see your child, not just any child who resembles yours. Your child, in this sense, is irreplaceable and cannot be duplicated – unlike the whisky.

The replaceable–irreplaceable distinction does not coincide

	Replaceable	Non-replaceable
Physical objects	A whisky A lemon	This original score The watch he gave
Persons	A milkman A man? A woman?	Winthrop Melissa

with the object–person distinction. On the one hand, some objects are irreplaceable. You are searching for your father's particular watch, not just any resembling watch. You want to own the original score or painting, not a forgery, even if you cannot tell the difference. On the other hand, some people are replaceable. You just need a milkman to deliver the milk, not any milkman in particular – unless the milkman is your lover. Lovers usually fit on the irreplaceable side of the divide. It is Winthrop that you love. If he has an identical twin, it is still for Winthrop that you yearn. When Winthrop is absent, you do not usually make do with the twin. Mind you, you may just want a man – or a woman. Then anyone, of the right looks, charm, stamina or whatever, will do.

*   *   *

Irreplaceability highlights the importance of how certain relationships develop. The lovers first met under the drinks' table at the birthday party and, from then on, their lives intertwined. The particular causal history of their relationship cannot be duplicated.

None of this gives any sense to there being a 'self' or 'essence' that lovers love, independently of the beloved's characteristics. At best, it suggests a wild optimism that the intertwining of the lovers' lives ensures that the changes in the lovers' characteristics will match, going hand in happy hand. Perhaps there is a suspension of belief about the contingencies and flux of the world, about the reductions in sexual desire for the familiar and about the differences between the sexes' emotional developments. We seek to live within a fictional world in which, to use a picture offered by Plato, lovers are those who have been reunited after an earlier division. It is when things go wrong that we warm to a quip such as 'Marriage is not a word but a sentence.'

When we attend a play, we can lose ourselves within the action. Despite awareness of the theatrical surroundings, we cannot help being moved by the characters on stage. My suggestion is that such fictionalism spills over those in love, generating an erotic fictionalism. When in love, we often cannot help feeling, and believing in, the eternity of that love, despite knowing that, transient and fickle creatures that we are, things may be so very, very different later on; even as early on as the following morning.

Mind you, I am a man.

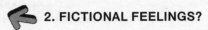 **2. FICTIONAL FEELINGS?**

13. WOLVES, WHISTLES AND WOMEN

23. UNIQUELY WHO?

30. EYE SPY

9

SAND, SUN, SEA AND . . .

Bikini-clad Sandy stretches out on hot sands, idly reflecting on their vastness. 'How many grains on this beach?' she wonders. 'Many more than one thousand.' But her eyesight alone is not sufficiently discerning to distinguish between one thousand and one thousand-and-one grains, unless she starts counting. Sandy, being but human, is unable to see the difference between a large number of grains and that number with one more added or one taken away – purely by looking, as opposed to, for example, popping them, one by one, into an urn and counting.

'I can tell, just from looking around me, that there are more than a thousand grains. Just by looking, I cannot spot the difference between a thousand and a thousand with one grain more, so I must be able to tell, on the basis of what I see and my bit of reasoning, that there are more than one thousand-and-one grains.' Thus, Sandy moves from the truth that there are at least one

thousand grains to the truth of there being at least one thousand-and-one.

'So, I know that there are at least one thousand-and-one grains, but I cannot tell the difference between that and one thousand-and-two, merely from looking; so I know that there are at least one thousand-and-two.' Sandy continues thus, going on, grain by grain, into the higher thousands. Of course, at these low numbers, she can tell, without any of the reasoning, that the beach has more grains than such low numbers of grains. After a while however, some uncertainty would cut in, unless she deployed and was convinced by the line of reasoning just outlined. And the reasoning, going up one grain at a time, would lead her to the millions, billions, trillions, trillion trillions and even the number which is the number of electrons in the whole universe, as being at least the number of grains on the beach. Somewhere *en route* she would have moved from truth to falsehood, for even though the beach is big and sandy, the grains do not reach the trillion trillions. Where does this reasoning go wrong?

A couple of grains of sand, every now and then, are blown off a nearby sandcastle, yet a couple of grains cannot make the difference between a sandcastle and a mere sandy mound. Remove a couple of grains and it would surely remain a castle; remove a couple more and it must surely remain a castle — and yet? Somewhere, if continued, that reasoning goes wrong, for it could leave us insisting that the castle remains when there is no castle left at all. Furthermore, Sandy is aware that she would be unable to distinguish the castle as it is right now from the same castle with a few grains missing. Remove a couple of grains and she will see it is a castle still. Remove a couple more and she must surely still see it is a castle — and yet . . .

A rock's shadow darkens her thighs. Twenty minutes earlier the shadow had only touched her toes. Even had she paid careful attention, she would not have noticed the shadow's gradual movement during one minute. Although she cannot spot the shadow's movement each minute, somehow she spots it over twenty; yet the twenty consists of twenty non-spotting temporal spans. She now notices how much closer the lapping waves are to her feet; yet she failed to detect the slight changes of their drawing closer.

A man stares at her. Her bikini top has slid off her breasts. It must have been gradually slipping; yet neither she nor the man could have spotted the teeny movement of skimpy material each second. Of course, they spot the cumulative effect. Sandy is excited, until she takes in the man's official uniform. She is on a puritan beach and, via imperceptible stages, has moved from decency to indecency. She is prepared to pay the fine but then realizes, from the man's gaze, that there may be an alternative . . .

If teeny changes make no difference, how can big changes make a difference when big changes are just collections of teeny ones?

The motif in our tales derives from the Greek philosopher Eubulides, who reflected that a heap of pebbles is still a heap even after one pebble is removed. First find a heap: remove a pebble and a heap remains. As it is still a heap, when we remove another pebble it remains a heap. Perform as many pebbling removals as you wish; according to this reasoning, we keep a heap — yet manifestly we do not. Similar reasoning should lead us mistakenly to conclude that the sandcastle remains a castle, however many grains are blown off.

Before saying that none of this matters, reflect on biological examples. Minute by minute a foetus develops, leading to baby, child, adult — with resultant different permissible treatments, moral treatments about which there are extremely strong disagreements. Even Sandy's move from decency to (perceived) indecency has significant consequences for her — and others.

The puzzle rests on some objects and concepts lacking sharp boundaries. At which point (if any) does a sandcastle cease to be a sandcastle? Let us acknowledge that there are grey areas concerning such sandy matters; but must there then not be sharp boundaries between the clear and the grey areas? It would seem not: so how do clear cases transform into the less clear? How can a grain of sand make a difference between what is a definite sandcastle and a vague or grey borderline sandcastle? These sandy slopes are slippery slopes.

There is also the question of what we know and how we perceive: witness Sandy and the lapping waves, moving shadow and number of grains making up the beach. Sandy cannot spot the difference, by feeling or sight, between the extent of the shadow cast on her thigh from one second to the next; yet, after repeated seconds, she notices that shadowy movements have occurred. She cannot sense a small slide of her bikini top; yet further small slides enable her to be aware of her topless state. If the small changes make no noticeable difference to her, how do they somehow add up to a noticeable difference? If a grain's difference cannot affect what she knows and can see, how can added unnoticed differences make a difference to what she knows and can see? How can she be justified in switching from judging that the pile of sand is a sandcastle, to hesitating a little, hesitating more, then to being certain that it is no sandcastle at all, when a single grain difference goes unnoticed?

*   *   *

I often know how to do something without knowing quite how I do it. I know how to cycle, open an awkward gate and drink a glass of wine, without knowing quite how I do these things. Some golfers just 'know' how to hole the ball without being able to explain how. People who have 'blind sight' sincerely report that they cannot see anything beyond a certain edge, yet give correct descriptions (more often than randomness would dictate) of what lies beyond that edge, without anything further to go on than what they, so to speak, 'cannot see'.

We speak of what Sandy can and cannot discern, yet we need to recognize that she can discern things without knowing that she can or how she can. Teeny changes, be they to do with sand, shadowy movements or bikini tops, are below Sandy's conscious awareness and hence imperceptible to her (if perceptibility demands awareness); but that does not mean that they do not register on her central nervous system. We detect some small changes without knowing that we do. This raises questions of how small neural changes, each of which leaves no conscious mark, eventually give rise to conscious awareness; and how some teeny changes in sandcastles affect the eye and optic nerve and brain while other teeny changes do not.

These thoughts offer no direct answer to how we manage to use vague terms — except to remind us that what we cannot consciously detect, we may yet be able to detect without conscious awareness. That there is some such detection explains why, at certain stages, we start hesitating about whether the castle is still a castle, whether the shadow is in the same position and whether the bikini slippage now exposes us — well, Sandy — to an indecency charge and fine.

 6. IN THE BEGINNING

18. VOTE! VOTE! VOTE?

23. UNIQUELY WHO?

25. I SHOT THE SHERIFF

10

MARY, MARY, QUITE CONTRARY

Whenever possible, Mary will do something different from what you expect. If she is deciding whether to take her holiday next week and you point out all the good reasons for her so to do, concluding that she is therefore bound to take the holiday – well, Mary will perversely stay at home. 'Mary, you'd doubtless like a cool drink; it's such a hot day.' Not much of a chance; she may well go for steaming hot tea. Mary, Mary, is, indeed, quite contrary. And Mary likes being contrary – to show you, to show all of us, that she is free. She is free to choose what to do, however irrational, however well we all know her. She may think that deciding to act irrationally shows that, unlike timers, thermostats and tea-making machinery, she and others possess free will.

For her knowingly to do the contrary, Mary needs to be told what you predict. If you predict that she will act somewhat per-versely and tell her so, she will do the opposite. Naturally, there are some things outside Mary's power or so dangerous that she will not make your prediction false. When you tell her that she will continue to breathe over the next ten minutes, she is not so silly as to undermine that.

Many philosophers – also neurologists, geneticists and psychologists – believe that all our actions are ultimately caused and are, indeed, determined by outside factors. Even if indeterminacy reigns at the quantum level much discussed by physicists, statistical laws hold firm. There is, indeed, increasing evidence that, away from the quantum and at the level of human interactions with the world, our actions are causally determined by factors beyond our control. These factors include our genetic characteristics, our conditioning as we grow up, the culture within which we live – and direct impingings of the environment upon our senses. In one way or another, these bring about our desires, speech, movements and much more; hence, it is exceedingly difficult to find any room for what is usually thought of as free will or free choice. In sum, what we do is determined by our nature and nurture, neither of which we choose.

In slightly more detail, Mary's actions – the movements she makes, the words she utters – are caused by electrochemical changes in her brain which themselves are caused by other electrochemical changes and impingings via her senses, and so on. Were scientists to know everything about genes, about how brains work and how they are affected by the environment, and about Mary's particular circumstances, they could predict everything that Mary, even Mary in contrary mode, would do. The scientists could place their predictions of Mary's behaviour in a sealed envelope and Mary would be unable to undermine those predictions. This would seem to show that Mary is not free and, for that matter, not free, whether or not anyone bothers to do the predicting.

But . . . but . . . but . . . Does not the following possibility remain? Were the scientists to make their predictions and were Mary to learn what they predict, is she not free to decide not to do what they have predicted? If they predict that she will choose the red dress, then she can choose whether to make their prediction false. She could go for the blue.

Are we not free to undermine predictions based on all the facts about us?

Acting contrary to what people expect of us – even what scientists predict about us – may seem to show that we are free. Mary's contrariness vividly brings this home. But is that freedom mere illusion? It is true that, typically, Mary can act otherwise than as people predict, but given her neural networks, she cannot act otherwise than as those networks cause.

If scientists tell Mary about their predictions, that is a causal input that will affect her neurological happenings; and so, those predictions may well affect what she does. Suppose we are the scientists who have learned all there is to know about her neurological states to date. We make our prediction of what she is going to do; whether she will choose the red dress or the blue. If we *tell* her that we predict the red, we need to take that feedback into account. In principle, it should be possible to anticipate how that feedback will affect Mary if thus fed back. On some occasions, we may know that, if she learns of our prediction, she will then act differently from what is predicted. Let this be such an occasion; let us see what happens.

We know that if we tell her of our red dress prediction (call this 'Prediction One'), she will choose the blue dress – and may even think this shows how free she is. We could secretly have predicted that of her (call this 'Prediction Two'). If she learns of Prediction Two – 'Mary will choose the blue because we told her we predicted the red' – we know that she will revert to red. That would generate Prediction Three, a prediction of which we are confident, unless Mary learns of it. If she does, we know how that will affect her and how she will respond. That could lead us to make Prediction Four, which would turn out correct, so long as she does not learn about it. And so on – with more and more predictions about how she will respond, given the inputs of the previous predictions.

This shows that, were we to learn all there is to learn about Mary and were all her actions completely determined, on some occasions we may know that it is impossible for her to learn of our correct predictions and they remain correct. It would also seem to show that Mary cannot learn all there is to know about herself such that she correctly predicts her own actions, yet is able to choose to act otherwise. This may be marked by the big distinction between our intending to do something and our merely predicting that we shall do it.

Maybe all there is to free will is the mere feeling and true belief that we would sometimes have acted differently from what was predicted, if told of the predictions; but it does not follow that we could have acted differently, given the particular causal inputs on us that remain outside our control.

*　　*　　*

The problem of free will and determinism haunts many people. I have suggested that acting freely is not possible, if all our actions are events that are determined, enmeshed in deterministic causal chains of events, with the causes stretching back into the past, before our birth and hence beyond our command. However, consider the alternative. Suppose that, after looking through brochures, discussing with friends and reflecting alone, I choose to holiday in Bucharest rather than Budapest. As with many free choices, I have my reasons for the choice. However, had that choice been causally determined, then – we are told – it would not be a genuine free choice. The alternative to the causal story is that such causal determination is lacking. My choice would then amount to being causally random – at least, that would seem to be how it came about, whatever I say about my reasons.

To act freely, however, is not to act randomly. Typically, we are held to account for what we freely do but if our choices and actions result, in some way, from randomness, we should not usually be so held. If our choices and actions come about randomly, then they seem to be as much beyond our control as choices and actions resulting from causal chains extending to times before we even existed. Whether our choices and actions are caused or random, what scope is there for making sense of what is surely so: namely, that we often act, freely act, on the basis of reasons?

The resulting bafflement should lead us to examine more carefully what we are seeking, when seeking the subject, the 'I', that does the choosing, deciding or acting, and that gives reasons for the choices, decisions and actions. If 'I' lacks all characteristics and character, as Jean-Paul Sartre seemed to think, then what we are talking about is baffling. It is also baffling how whatever it is that we are talking about could make choices at all, including, therefore, any choices of what characteristics and character to develop, as well as what actions to perform. If characteristics and character are granted to 'I', then we naturally look for causes outside the 'I' which brought about those characteristics and character. Whichever way we approach the matter, we fail to find anything like the free choices, decisions and actions which we apparently want, namely ones which are ours, under our exclusive control and for which, indeed, we can usually give reasons. We are left bewildered – as bewildered as we are when reading Sartre who seems to claim that it is our nothingness that somehow enables us to make free choices.

A common response to the bewilderment is that 'acting freely' is more to do simply with our getting what we want or having *our* reasons for what we do, without reference to neurological causal stories. This would indeed be compatible with such actings being determined and within causal chains. Of course, the cry then goes up, 'But I am not free to choose my wants.' Well, on what basis would you choose them?

What is it that we choose? Well, the red underwear (oops!), *Seinfeld* DVD and a holiday in Venice. As scientists uncover more laws to explain movements, moods and tendencies to drink, do we expect laws of underwear, *Senfeld* and holidaying abroad? Let them predict Mary's eyelids' flutter, but is that an action of flirting, signalling a gin – or just a twitch?

As a footnote, let us note that arguments about whether our behaviour is explained by our genes or by our upbringing and environment are irrelevant to the problem of whether we act freely. Philosophically, it does not terribly matter which is more prominent. If the threat to freedom is having our actions caused by things outside our control, then, if indeed out of our control, it is irrelevant whether those things be genetic or environmental, nature or nurture.

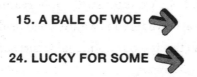

15. A BALE OF WOE

24. LUCKY FOR SOME

11

JUST HANGING AROUND

Logical Lo knew it was a mistake to holiday in Wild West parts, where cowboys and sheriffs were laws unto themselves – and to visitors. Here sits Lo, sentenced to death by hanging – a hanging with a twist, a very strange twist, in its noose. The sheriff had taken a dislike to her when she had rebuffed his advances, denounced him as sexist and danced a jig on his ten-gallon hat.

'Tis now Sunday. The sheriff has just announced to Lo that she is to be hanged, at noon, one day this coming week – either Monday, Tuesday, Wednesday, Thursday or Friday. Saturday is *siesta* day, when no one hangs around. The hanging will be a surprise: on the morning of the hanging, Lo will have no good reason to believe that the hanging will take place that day. Perhaps, for example, she will undergo the noonday noose on Tuesday: if so, on Tuesday morning (and before then) she will have no good reason to believe that the hanging will be on that day. Lo knows, she just knows, that the sheriff speaks the truth.

Things look bleak. Lo is too young to hang. Distraught, she settles in her cell, but then she starts to reason and reflect. After all, she is Logical Lo.

If I get through to Friday morning, unhung and hence unhanged, my neck still intact, then the hanging would have to occur that day at noon, for there are no other days left. So, for the hanging to be a surprise, it cannot occur on Friday. Friday is ruled out. Mind you, there are still all the other days.

Hold on — as Friday is ruled out for the hanging, then, if I get through unhanged to Thursday morning, I'd know the hanging would have to be on that day's noon. That's the only day left, given Friday is no real possibility; hence, I can rule out Thursday . . .

So Lo reasons, ruling out Friday, then Thursday, then Wednesday and so on down the days, ruling out Tuesday and Monday by similar reasoning. Smugly, she concludes that the sentence announced by the sheriff cannot be implemented. 'My neck is safe,' smirks Logical Lo, in confident mode, ravished by reason.

Then, one day that week, perhaps Wednesday or even Friday, the hangman intrudes upon Lo's confident complacency and hangs her. She is both hanged and surprised or, more accurately, surprised and hanged.

Surprise hangings, surprise parties, surprise school examinations, can be given, yet if both the spectrum of possible dates and the fact that the event will be a surprise are guaranteed, did Lo not prove that, paradoxically, such surprises cannot occur?

Where does Lo's argument, that there can be no surprise hanging, go wrong?

A natural way of handling the paradox is to point out that when someone is told of a surprise under such conditions — and schoolchildren often are given surprise examinations in this way, though currently not hangings – what is meant is that the event will be a surprise, *unless* it happens on the last possible day. If you have reached the last possible day, then obviously you will not be surprised, so the backward reasoning does not get started and the puzzle evaporates. It is then no more puzzling than being told that we shall be unable to work out which of four face down ace cards (Clubs? Diamonds? Hearts? Spades?) will be turned up last, until three have had their faces turned up; after three are shown, we may easily work out which ace remains unturned. The puzzle also is no puzzle if Lo knows that the sheriff could be having her on; for then possibly no hanging will take place. Once again, the backward reasoning cannot start. It starts once Lo believes that Friday is a possible day for the surprise hanging – for then, what can she conclude?

The puzzle bites if you have excellent reason to think the sheriff is telling the truth. If he is – and if you suppose you get through to Friday morning – then there is a conflict in your reasons for what to believe. He tells you that there will definitely be a hanging; hence, on Friday morning, you think that it must occur today (it is the last possible day). Yet he also tells you that it will be a surprise, so, now on Friday morning, you think his overall announcement cannot be true: maybe the hanging will not occur. But then you realize that you now are not believing that there will be a hanging; yet, in that state of mind, you can reflect that his overall announcement could well be true after all: you do not believe there will be a hanging, so now it can both occur and be a surprise. That reflection reels you round into again believing that a hanging will happen – but in that state of mind it will not be a surprise to you; and so you go through the reasoning again. Such reeling means that no stable belief can be reached. The reasoning loops round and round.

*   *   *

We should question whether Lo can have good reason to believe that the sheriff is right in predicting both that there will be a hanging and that she will not believe that there will be one, if she is left hanging around, unhanged, until Friday. How can the sheriff predict her state of mind? Perhaps he could for people who are unable to grasp the reasoning – but Logical Lo is logical, her reasoning both seemingly impeccable and also reeling her between thinking her neck will meet the noose and thinking it will be noose free. Hence the sheriff cannot know what she will believe just before a hanging on Friday and hence he cannot be certain that she will be surprised. Logical Lo, who will also have worked this out, should realize that she has no good reason to believe that the sheriff's announcement must be true with regard to both the hanging and its being a surprise.

To be true, the sheriff's announcement means that if she is left hanging around, unhanged, until Friday morning (or if she projects herself to Friday morning), she will think 'My hanging will take place at noon but I don't believe my hanging will take place at noon.' What she thinks has the same structure and absurdity as the thought in Moore's Paradox (yet to be discussed, with reference to Private Pike). Surprisingly, the puzzle neither results from the sheriff's telling Lo of the surprise hanging, nor from there being a surprise hanging, but from Lo's believing what the sheriff tells her.

14. DON'T TELL HIM, PIKE!

31. DON'T READ THIS NOTICE

12

IT'S ALL RELATIVE . . . ISN'T IT?

An adulteress is stoned to death – a slow, painful and humiliating death – in a country ruled under a version of *Sharia* law. In Britain today, no legal sanction is applied against adultery. Some people in Britain would consider her adultery immoral; others, possibly including her husband, would not see anything wrong. In Britain, Europe and elsewhere, the great, great majority of people would assess the punishment of stoning as horrendous and deeply wrong. Some say this shows that such matters are relative. What she did was wrong relative to her culture, yet not wrong or not so wrong, relative to modern Western culture. Relative to that country's Muslim morality and law, she was rightly punished.

Many years ago, in a school debate, I spoke in favour of the motion 'Down with the mini skirt!' Supporting the motion enabled me to engage in the schoolboy humour of the *double entendre* 'down with'. At the time, miniskirts were fashionable;

a few years later they were out. Fashions come and go – as do words for the fashionable – 'chic', 'cool', 'groovy', 'trendy', 'wicked', 'with it'. What we find attractive, daring, acceptable or offensive is relative to its context. Once, it is said, men swooned at the glimpse of a lady's ankle. Consider how red wine tasted to you as a child (nasty?) with how it tastes now. Contrast the reactions to grilled canine *bleu* served in Korea with those to the same dish served in Britain; to sexual relationships involving boys in ancient Athens with those to such relationships in the West today; or the reactions of Scots to bagpipe music with those of the English to such noise – I mean, sounds.

Cultural relativists typically extend such relativities to morality. What is morally right or wrong is, they claim, relative to society. Expansive relativists (as I term them) expand relativity further, some even to all truths. They say, for example, 'God exists' is true for believers but false for non-believers; or 'the Earth is flat' was true for most people in the Middle Ages but is not true for us now. They may argue that when I try to say that something is true absolutely – that is, not relatively – all I am doing is saying what I believe. I cannot get out of my own skin and find out how things really are. Some relativists argue that there is no 'really are' at all. It's all relative.

Are all values and truths relative?

Relativism, arguably, seems more persuasive when the seem-ing truths are to do with morality – with what we morally ought or ought not to do – than when those seeming truths are to do with the world around us. Moral relativism is supported by many Western secularists. Such relativists, considering the stoning discussed above, sometimes mistakenly infer that it is wrong for us to interfere with the practices of that other country. If that conclusion is put forward as a non-relative claim, namely, that interfering is wrong 'full stop', then it contradicts the relativists' claim that all moral judgements are relative. Such relativists cannot consistently hold to their position. That is a clear reason to reject *their* relativism.

Perhaps moral relativists are saying that it is wrong, relative to a group's values (presumably, their group's), to interfere with another's country's (relative) values. If that is the story, I may find it interesting but, as it is only a relative matter, on its own it provides me with no good reason to accept their values.

Although relativism may seem naturally to go with a liberal toleration – as far as possible, do not interfere with others – there is no good reason why. Relativists cannot coherently tell nations, sects or individuals that they are wrong 'full stop' when they impose their values on others, for those nations, sects or individuals may well value the spreading of their (relative) values to others. That all moral judgements are relative does not justify our drawing the conclusion, even if taken relatively, that therefore we in this country ought not to interfere with the practices of another country, just as it does not justify drawing the conclusion that therefore we ought to interfere in the practices of another country.

Once morality is taken to be relative, there is the question: relative to what? To the society in which we live? To sub-groups – sects, political parties, unions, clubs – to which we belong? To some other authority? To me? Whatever the answer, we should then ask the relativists: is your answer just relatively true, that is, just true for you or your group? If it is, why should I pay attention to it? If not, then you are no true relativists.

Students sometimes profess a belief in relativism. They confront the folly of their professing when it is pointed out that if they are right, they ought not to complain that it is wrong for me to give them low marks. 'Our essays are good,' they insist. 'Absolutely,' say I, 'but as absolute non-relative values do not exist, your essays deserve low marks, relative to how I feel right now.'

Many left-wing radicals are drawn towards moral relativism because they want to respect other people's cultural identities. This leads them into the quagmire of trying to square their relativism with their judgement (surely correct) that women ought not to be forced to be veiled, undergo genital mutilation or be literally stoned to death. Of course, let me hasten to add, there are many ills in Western societies: women often feel pressured into having children, having a man or, indeed, having no man at all.

Respect for culture and tradition ought not to be taken to imply that all cultures and traditions should be respected. Such respect does imply that some respects are right absolutely, not merely relatively. A puzzle is where to draw the lines or, in fact, where to find the lines drawn.

*   *   *

The ancient Greek sophist, Protagoras, is seen as the key source for fully expanded expansive relativism. 'Man is the measure of all things,' he said. His position seems to be that what is true is always a matter of what is true *for* someone. There is no such thing as truth full stop. A quick (and correct) response is to wonder about the status of Protagoras' claim – just as we should wonder about the status of any argument put forward to defend relativism. 'All truths are relative.' Is that relative or non-relative? If the latter, then it is self-refuting, so we should reject it. If the former, if it merely means, 'For me, Protagoras, all truth is relative,' we should answer, 'That is all very well Mr Protagoras, but why should we take any notice of what you say? After all, you're only talking about how things strike you, not how they are.'

Mr Protagoras stamps his feet and shouts, 'But I am the great Protagoras who has thought about these things and who has seen . . .' At this he hesitates – what he needs to say to influence us he cannot consistently say; for he needs to say that his arguments are better than others' and not merely relatively so for him. He needs to be saying that he has seen . . . er . . . er . . . the truth. Full stop.

Place a moral relativist in front of a screaming, innocent child being tortured. Ask her if she still thinks that what is being done is only relatively wrong.

Place an expansive relativist on the tracks before an advancing express train. Ask her if she really does think that it is only relatively true that she is about to die.

21. SAINTS, SINNERS AND SUICIDE BOMBERS

22. A BIT RICH

31. DON'T READ THIS NOTICE

13

WOLVES, WHISTLES AND WOMEN

Butchers, bakers and candlestick makers – or, for that matter, nurses, judges and street cleaners – do not, typically, rail at being used as (if I may introduce the term) 'job objects'. Yet some women, especially those bedecked in feminist clothing, rail and rage against being treated as *sex* objects. They argue that men frequently (if not always) regard them thus, at work, in the street and even in bed. Men are wolves, ever ready to pounce on women as meat to be violated and devoured. Indeed, where sexual relations are concerned it seems that woman is but:

> An object of appetite; as soon as that appetite has been stilled, she is cast aside as one casts away a lemon which has been sucked dry . . . all motives of moral relationship cease to function, because as an object of appetite she becomes a thing and can be treated as such by everyone.

Curiously, this quotation derives – admittedly with some modifications – not from an obvious extreme feminist but from the great eighteenth-century German philosopher, Immanuel Kant. I have modified his comment as if it were directed solely towards the sexual treatment of women but Kant did not discriminate: to him, both men and women are treated as objects in the sexual relation. We use each other solely as means to our ends; when the ends are just sexual pleasures, we degrade each other into mere instruments.

Human love – goodwill, affection and concern for the other's happiness – comes to the rescue. When sexual love is combined with human love, within heterosexual marriage, things are better. The marriage contract gives the contracting partners equal rights to the life-long reciprocal use of the other's sexual organs and capacities. Yes, it has, unfortunately, to be admitted that the sexually abstemious Kant writes in unromantic terms, as if sexual desire is solely for the use of our and the other's genitals.

It is not just bedtime that troubles some women (and, of course, men). In the street, at work or at play, some women feel they are assessed primarily as sex objects rather than people. It has been said that women live in sexual objectification the way in which fish live in water. Yet, even if sexual objectification is not so pervasive, some women are still distressed when it is present. The distress is rather puzzling: we frequently use people, yet they do not thereby see themselves as misused or taken as objects. Further, where sex is concerned,

many women and men value accolades based on their sexual attractiveness.

What is all the fuss about being treated as sex objects?

Being a sex object is usually written about in terms of women as the objects of men's desires. Mistreatment is likely also to arise in homosexual and other relationships but – for simplicity – let us stay with heterosexuals. There is the basic, empirical, question of whether women typically are treated as sex objects. Various features cluster round 'sex object'. It sometimes involves being treated merely as a tool for others' use or pleasure. Sometimes there is the idea that the woman's experiences and free choices matter not at all; sometimes that she is treated as if lacking free will, rationality and interests; sometimes that it is acceptable for her to be violated. Sometimes there is stress on her being replaceable – that anyone with her sexual characteristics would do. This clustering makes it difficult to give simple answers to this question. Let us consider some comparisons.

Male builders wolf-whistle at an attractive woman walking by, purely on the basis of her sexual allure. She is not treated as a person but as sexual flesh on legs, replaceable by any other piece of like or better quality. This example (frequently given) may also be taken as insensitively identifying some people as job objects; builders are, in part, employed on the basis of their physical characteristics – they are replaceable and often replaced. Taxi-drivers are whistled at for their taxi-driving and, if the first cab is taken, the second will do. These are, however, poor analogies: being a woman is not an occupation and walking by is not usually indicative of an occupational role. Further, builders and taxi-drivers are not being regarded merely as means but also as ends. They are seen as people who have voluntarily taken up their occupation (how voluntarily is a matter for another discussion); in using them we are promoting their own perceived interests.

Caveats and responses are required. Typically we do – and should – treat taxi-drivers as people and not as added pieces of taxi-machinery, but we initially select them on their physical proximity (charges or driving skills). We choose builders because of their muscles and abilities as builders, but do not thereby treat them as objects. When a woman is whistled at because of her curves, it does not follow that, in any resulting relationship, she would be treated purely as a thing curved. Even women have been known to fall in love at first sight; yet we should not conclude that they would treat the men sighted as nothing but objects that manifest whichever features proved so visually desirable. Identifying people by their bodies, being attracted by their physical features, employing them for their muscular prowess or consulting them for their reasoning powers, should not lead us to think that therefore we are bound to deal with them as nothing more than bodies, sets of physical characteristics, brawny muscles or reasoners.

The 'sex object' complaint is *sometimes* well-justified. Consider cases when a woman's sexual desirability forms the basis for job promotion judgements that should be made on other grounds. Consider cases when women, hurrying to work, are badgered because of their sexual desirability. Consider cases when oppressive male gazes make women feel vulnerable.

Even here, caveats need to be entered. No one seriously thinks that the way many men and women dress has nothing to do with displaying sexual attractiveness or improving the prospects of promotion. No one seriously thinks that, in social situations – be they work, be they play – many women and men do not enjoy being found desirable. It can be fun (so I hear). The problem is assessing when flirtations, invitations and innuendoes are appropriate. Some women are pleased to receive whistles – as are some men.

*   *   *

What should we make of the 'sex object' complaint, related to the throes of sexual passion?

Sexual relations are often mundane, yet often they involve a medley of activities. Typically, neither men nor women seek inactive *objects* as sexual partners. During sex, if things go well, we are made highly aware of our embodied state, through our and our partner's arousal, which may then heighten further mutual arousals; a kaleidoscope of experiences. That leads some to stress a mysterious interplay between being aware of ourselves and our partners as conscious experiencing subjects, while trying to make each other nothing but flesh. However, some feminist writers see an essential asymmetry. Men are bound to dominate; penetration is akin to a violence, a brutality, an occupation to which women surrender. Indeed, it can be; but we could equally use metaphors of men being enveloped, smothered, devoured, losing themselves and succumbing. Certain feminist writers seem unaware of the consent that usually occurs between sexual partners, including consent to sado-masochistic activity. They also sometimes appear oblivious to the distinction that usually exists between the sexual activities of female prostitutes and their male clients and those of couples engaged in mutual arousal.

With increasing interest in the fetish scene and sado-masochistic sex, perhaps we should resist the generalized, woolly and misleading talk of sex objects – talk which perpetuates notions of woman as victim. Perhaps we should pay more attention to the good old Liberty Principle of John Stuart Mill, in which whatever people get up to among themselves, including sex, should be permitted so long as it is consensual and directly harms no one else without his or her consent.

In sexual relations, women and men, in various numbers and packages, consent to all manner of things. Before feminists challenge the authenticity of the woman's consent, it is worth commenting that it is no more likely to be right that, when women say 'yes', they do not mean yes than it is that, when women say 'no', they do not really mean no.

 8. WILL YOU STILL LOVE ME TOMORROW?

17. GIRL, CAGE, CHIMP

14

DON'T TELL HIM, PIKE!

In the BBC television series, *Dad's Army*, a part-time British Home Guard platoon helps defend Britain in World War II. The local bank manager, Mainwaring, is the platoon's pompous captain. Pike is a young and gullible private. No doubt by mistake, the platoon is holding captive a few German soldiers. After Pike makes some offensively childish remarks, the English-speaking German leader demands that Pike reveal his name, so that he can be dealt with when the Third Reich secures victory. Quick as a flash, Captain Mainwaring shouts across – in front of the listening enemy – 'Don't tell him, Pike!'

The scene is one of British television's most popular for comedy. Part of the humour derives from Mainwaring's attempt to ensure that the enemy is not informed of Pike's name – by means which ensure the enemy is so informed.

Although Mainwaring does not *state* that the private's name is 'Pike', his use of Pike's name in telling the young man to keep quiet gives the name and hence the game away. His action is *contra* his intended *diction*. His action is enemy informative, whereas his purpose is to render the enemy uninformed. His instruction gives rise to an informational absurdity.

Now for something which may seem to be completely different. Consider the following statement about my good friend, Zoe: 'Riga is the capital of Latvia but Zoe doesn't think it is.' The first part, about Riga, is true and is conjoined to a second part, about Zoe's view on the matter (and let us assume that that is indeed her view). Now, let Zoe try to tell us the same truth: 'Riga is the capital of Latvia but I don't think it is.' We are both saying the same about Riga and, it seems, about Zoe's view on the matter: what she thinks or believes. What comes from my lips is sensible but from Zoe's it is absurd. Try getting yourself into the position of sincerely asserting that something is so-and-so, yet sincerely asserting also that you do not think it is so or do not believe it is so.

There are exceptions. Sometimes no absurdity arises: you may, so to speak, be speaking with two voices. As train announcer, you say 'The train will be on time' yet softly add, 'I don't think it will.' 'I don't believe it' can also be a way of expressing surprise: 'I won the lottery but I still don't believe it!'

How can saying something true be absurd?

In 1940s Cambridge, G. E. Moore presented the puzzle in terms of belief. Wittgenstein highlighted its significance, claiming that it showed that my relation to my own words is wholly different from other people's to those words. We may readily talk about Zoe's psychological states, using expressions such as 'Zoe thinks this,' or 'She doesn't believe that,' but when Zoe is speaking, in the first person, present tense, for example saying 'I think Wittgenstein gave away his inheritance,' she is not describing her psychological state; rather, she is expressing, with some hesitation, something about Wittgenstein.

Consider this case. It is raining and you are wondering whether it is worth waiting for a bus. A woman at the bus stop discusses this with you and finally says, 'I'm certain the bus will be here in a few minutes.' After some time with no bus, you challenge her, pointing out that she had got things wrong and had misled you, presumably unintentionally. It would not go down well if she responded, 'I was merely telling you about my psychological state – my state of certainty, belief and what I firmly thought – not about the bus's likely arrival.'

Use of 'I think', 'I believe', 'I am certain' – and also, 'I don't think', 'I don't believe', 'I'm not sure' – is typically a means of expressing something about the world, with varying degrees of certainty or hesitation. Zoe's statement that seemed to be about both Riga and her lack of belief is more akin to her saying: 'Riga is the capital of Latvia but [hesitantly] Riga is not the

capital of Latvia.' The second part is Zoe speaking (albeit hesi-
tantly) against herself in the first part. Captain Mainwaring's
instruction generated an informational absurdity; so too does
Zoe's utterance.

*   *   *

The peculiarity that Moore noticed and Wittgenstein stressed
occurs with many first person present tense uses of psychological terms but not with past and future tense uses. 'Riga is the
capital of Latvia but I used not to believe so' is not absurd. A
feature of belief is that if you believe that something is so-and-
so, then you believe that it is true that that something is so-and-
so. Hence, there is no use, in the first person present tense, of
'falsely believing'. Maybe I falsely believed that Riga was the
capital of Hungary but I cannot sensibly say, 'I falsely believe
that Riga is the capital of Hungary,' though others can sensibly
say it of me.

The peculiarity of first person present tense uses has been
much explored since Wittgenstein, notably by J. L. Austin. 'I
name this ship *Matilda*' is to perform a naming, not merely to
describe what I am doing. 'I bet', 'I promise', 'I order' are further examples of what have become known as 'performatives'.

Consider, 'I assert that Riga is the capital of Hungary.' You
tell me that I am mistaken: Riga is not the capital of Hungary. I
reject your accusation of error. 'I merely said that I *assert* that
Riga is the capital of Hungary, not that Riga *is* the capital of
Hungary.' Is that a fair riposte? Is prefacing remarks with 'I

assert that . . .', as suggested in this book's preface, a way of always speaking the truth?

 4. HE WOULD SAY THAT, WOULDN'T HE?

31. DON'T READ THIS NOTICE

15

A BALE OF WOE

While wandering across centuries past, o'er hill and vale, came I upon an ass, so thin, so scraggy, that I felt concern, so overwhelming, for its health. 'Oh, Ass,' said I, 'you are so thin, so forlorn, so pale; why eat you not? Are you blind? There is, just here, right here, towards your left, a bale of hay – the straws are golden – and, with steps a few, that whole bale yours will easily be.' As I spoke, I noticed how his eyes swivelled repeatedly from left to right, from right to left.

'Kind sir,' replied Ass, 'would that things were as simple as that. Indeed, I can see that golden bale of succulent hay to my left so well but, can you not see? There is another bale, equally golden and with a degree of succulence the very same, exactly the same, to my right.'

'That is true,' replied I, 'but that is all the better – is it not? – for poor starving and skinny you. You have two bales upon

which to dine instead of one. Are they not equally tempting, my dear, dear Ass?'

'Precisely the problem, dear Sir,' moaned Ass, eyes ever swivelling between bundle left and bundle right. 'They are indeed equal in all their features, save one to my left does sit and, the other, my right. They are equal in succulence, in weight, in size, in goldenness, in all respects indeed. They're the same distance away from me too.'

'Yes?' questioned I, looking baffled and lost, not least because baffled and lost was I.

'You see,' sighed Ass, 'I need a reason for choosing to eat one rather than t'other — but I have no reason. The bundles are equally attractive, so equally so.'

'Eat both!' I snapped, teenily tired of Ass's bleak groans.

'Don't be angry with me, Sir. I am an ass of reason. I need a reason for choosing which to eat first.' And as he brayed, he visibly weakened yet further, still further, with hunger, so weak was he, so weak.

'Well, act without reason,' declared I.

'Sir, rational beings need reasons for actions. What else could motivate them?' came his woeful reply.

'Hunger,' I muttered but, by then, I knew reasoning with Ass was foolish. He was a fine and upstanding ass, despite falling to the ground, moaning most pitifully, yet courteously. Action was required. I would bring just one of the bundles right up to him, so he would have a reason to eat of that first, for it would require no walk, unlike the other bundle that would remain in place some distance from him.

My eyes swivelled from left to right and right to left and suddenly I realized that I could not decide which bundle to fetch.

Do we always need a reason for choosing one course of action rather than another?

Jean Buridan, a French medieval logician, is linked to this puzzle; hence it is traditionally known as 'Buridan's Ass'. Centuries after Buridan, Leibniz put forward his principle of sufficient reason, his 'apex of rationality'. There must be a sufficient reason for everything that happens, including what we do. Incidentally, Leibniz uses the principle to argue for the existence of a being that necessarily exists, namely God. God's necessary existence is the only reason that is sufficient – enough – to explain the existence of the universe. What is the sufficient reason for God's existence? Well, he necessarily exists and so he is his own sufficient reason.

Buridan's Ass has more ramifications than are usually recognized. Suppose I had managed to give Ass just one bundle: he would still need to choose which straw to bite into first. True, one straw may be a little closer or thicker than the other but would that be sufficient reason to choose one over the other? It is not just a matter of finding a difference between the alternatives – the original bundles had different locations; one to the left, the other to the right – but of finding a difference that is relevant to what we want. Is it true that, to be rational, we need a sufficient and relevant reason for everything that we do?

The answer is that we can, and often should, act without reason. To be rational, we should on some occasions act irrationally, or, better, non-rationally, that is, without a reason for every feature of the actions performed. Ass has a splendid and sufficient reason to eat – to avoid starvation – and that is sufficient reason to eat either the left bale or the right. His mistake is to think that he also needs sufficient reason for choosing either the left bale over the right or the right over the left.

*   *   *

This answer may yet be inadequate, if we think of reasons as motivating forces – the oomphs! – that get us moving. Without a reason for choosing the left rather than the right (or vice versa) we lack the oomph to get our legs stepping off one way rather than the other. This is, though, to mistake reasons for causes. We may certainly wonder about which events cause our bodily movements and how they are related to the reasons that we give. We may be inclined to believe that everything that we do has causes and those causes have causes. It is possible that two bales are sufficiently similar that they have the same causal effects on us, causing neurological changes such that we equally incline towards the left as towards the right, leading to a paralysis such as Ass's. As Spinoza quipped, we should be asinine to be in that position: being human, we can still choose, even when choices are equally balanced in significance. Or can we?

Try this. When you next are unable to choose between alternatives, yet you have to do something, what happens and how does it happen?

27. CHICKEN! CHICKEN! CHICKEN!

 11. JUST HANGING AROUND

32. MYSTERIES

16

JUST HELPING OURSELVES

Here are a few words, courtesy of John Aubrey, about Thomas Hobbes, the seventeenth-century political philosopher. People often warm to Hobbes when they read them.

> He was very charitable (to the best of his ability) to those that were true objects of his bounty. One time, I remember, going in the Strand, a poor and infirmed old man craved his alms. He, beholding him with eyes of pity and compassion, put his hand in his pocket and gave him six pence. Said a divine (Dr Jaspar Mayne) that stood by: 'Would you have done this, if it had not been Christ's command?' 'Yea,' said he. 'Why?' quoth the other. 'Because,' said he, 'I was in pain to consider the miserable condition of the old man and now my alms, giving him some relief, doth also ease me.'

The moral often drawn from such tales is that we never act other than out of self-interest, that is, selfishly. It is true that sometimes we help others but this is only to ease our distress at seeing them in distress – it is our distress that ultimately motivates us.

The suggested story is that all our actions, despite contrary appearances, are really self-interested or selfish. The mother who runs into a burning house to save her child is motivated by fear; fear of how she would feel if she let her child die. Saints who sacrifice their lives, defending their Christian beliefs, are motivated by desire for an afterlife in heaven rather than hell. Atheists who, 'out of duty', volunteer to help the homeless really just want to feel good about themselves and perhaps impress their neighbours.

The ultimate consideration, if we dare to challenge the above, is that when we perform any action, we must have some motivation – and that means that, in some sense, we want to do it and so we act to satisfy that want. But if we are doing something to satisfy our wants, then we are acting selfishly. That is the catch-all argument. What we want may not coincide with what is in our own interests, so the reasoning needs, more accurately, to speak of how we always act in accordance with what we want or what we *take* to be our own self-interest.

Is it possible to do anything that is not, in some way, self-interested?

Various philosophical puzzles rely on views about what is 'really' the case. Curiously, students – and some philosophers – once in philosophy seminars, seem quickly to come to know or apprehend what is *really* so, even though this differs radically from what is reckoned to be really so outside the seminar room. It takes very little reflection to lead certain philosophers and students into believing that we never 'really' know anything much, can never 'really' be certain of much and are not 'really' free – even though it seems that, in our everyday lives, we frequently can tell whether someone knows something, is certain of something and did something freely.

What are we to make of the claim that 'really' we never act solely out of concern for others? It may be an empirical claim, one that we assess on the evidence around us, yet if that is so, it looks to be false: people certainly seem, on occasions, to act purely out of concern for others. The self-interest claim, though, is often put forward in such a way that it *cannot* be refuted. Whatever examples we give of selfless actions, the response is, 'Ah, so if she did X, it must have been because really she wanted to do X – and so she was self-interested after all.' It looks as if altruism and acting solely for the benefit of others have been ruled out of existence – for just wanting to do these things is sufficient to show that the person doing them is not altruistic but selfish.

Some years ago, I saw Mrs Thatcher, then Prime Minister, being interviewed about a hospital crisis: nurses were going on strike. At one point, Mrs Thatcher said, 'But nurses do not strike.' The interviewer was flabbergasted. He pointed out that there, on screen, were pictures of nurses in Trafalgar Square, waving banners, announcing that they were striking. 'Ah,' replied Mrs Thatcher, 'they're not true nurses.' What had started off as a claim about the world which could be investigated, an empirical claim – the claim that nurses do not strike – became in Mrs Thatcher's worded worldly ways a claim made true come what may. No one would be allowed to count as being a nurse, if she or he went on strike.

The move – from an interesting empirical claim to one made true by linguistic fiat – is arguably at work when people tell us that all our actions are really self-interested. If it is an empirical claim, let us test it. Is it the case that mothers rush to save their children only through fear of their own future distress? Why believe that? Is it true that if anyone sacrifices his life for a cause, he is really doing it for his own benefit? Why believe that? If there is evidence that shows these things, let us see it, but let us not use the theory (plucked from where?) that all actions are self-interested to conclude that any seemingly altruistic action must really – even unconsciously – be selfish.

*   *   *

Recently, there has been a tendency to move away from the level of people to that of genes, famously summed up by Richard Dawkins' book title *The Selfish Gene*. Of course, genes are not the kind of things that can be selfish and, if any metaphor is sought, 'vain' would be better, in so far as genes replicate themselves. Genetic considerations lead some to speak of altruism 'really' being a means for genes to increase their replication success. This is dangerous talk. Just because it is true that there are causal explanations (in terms of genes, replication and variation) for the existence of people with the range of features that they have, it does not follow that therefore no one is ever altruistically motivated. Just the reverse: the explanations are explanations of how it is that there is genuinely altruistic behaviour.

To load all human behaviour into the same selfish boat — maybe through tales of genetic explanations or unconscious motivations — blurs valuable distinctions between, for example, people who help you without any expectation of reward and those who help you only if there is a reward. Now, which sort would you prefer as your friends — or to meet, when you are stranded and lost, car broken down?

Insist, if you must, in moving the linguistic goalposts and thinking of all humans as selfish; but then you need to distinguish between those who help you for a fee and those who help you for free.

 10. MARY, MARY, QUITE CONTRARY

26. YOU'LL NEVER GET TO HEAVEN . . .?

22. A BIT RICH

27. CHICKEN! CHICKEN! CHICKEN!

17

GIRL, CAGE, CHIMP

Picture, if you will, a four-year-old girl in a cage. She has been captured, screaming; she saw her parents beaten off by the kidnappers. She rocks to and fro, showing obvious signs of fear and mental instability. It is unclear quite what is being done to her but some of the time she undoubtedly suffers physical pain. Wires are attached to a shaven portion of her head and, although she is given food and water, it looks as if some drugs are mixed in.

Perhaps I have asked you to picture a political torture camp. Maybe she has been placed under these stressful conditions to frighten her parents into confessing to political outrages. Perhaps I have asked you to picture a daughter who has been kidnapped and is being held to ransom. Or am I raising the question of whether picturing possesses moral dimensions?

Not at all. For my purposes, you are picturing a child actress, playing the part of a caged girl in *My Mate's A Primate*, a short

advertisement made by Animal Defenders International. Many
people, if they encounter such films, dismiss the scenes as fan-
tasies dreamt up by crazy animal liberationists. Some scientists,
such as those engaged in testing on animals, stress the unfair
emotional appeal: they speak of how well animals are cared for
when undergoing experimentation – adding, in truth, that they
are thereby safe from their usual predators. Many people are
shocked by the images of caged and frightened animals undergoing all kinds of testing. Some conclude that animal experimentation should be banned; others argue that such experimentation
is nasty but also necessary for the proper development of drugs
to benefit mankind – and even animal kind.

Our puzzle rests not on challenging the facts but on the consistency of those who argue in favour of animal testing. Assume that the favourers are right, that testing on live animals is needed for the development of safe drugs. Assume that the suffering caused by such testing is a necessary evil, far outweighed by the eventual benefits; for it would be irresponsible to distribute untested drugs to thousands of ill people. Note that such reasoning, in terms of overall consequences, is often deployed by people who are otherwise appalled at thinking about right and wrong in terms of consequences. Such people would usually speak of rights which should not be violated, however welcome the eventual consequences.

Here comes the puzzle. There are early stages of human lives in which the humans' emotional and intellectual awareness and their perspective on the world are less than those of (for example) adult chimps. Some claim that adult chimps possess the same mental and emotional development as four-year-old children – hence the particular film mentioned above. Whatever the exact age, whatever the animal, the question is:

Why is animal experimentation morally permissible if experimentation on children is not?

If the answer is simply that children are human, whereas chimps are not, the answerers are exposed to the charge of speciesism. They are discriminating between creatures purely on the basis of species' membership and that is akin to discriminating between people because of their race or sex. Such discrimination is unfair, unless some characteristics of that species, race or sex, can be shown to justify the difference in treatment.

We are not being sexist in providing prostate cancer screening for men but not for women. Obviously, a relevant male–female difference justifies the different treatment. Arguably, we are not speciesist when we kill sheep painlessly while rejecting the killing of humans. In killing sheep (in contrast to adult humans), we are not destroying individuals who possess a sense of continuing into the future, with plans, hopes and intentions. We are speciesist if we inflict suffering on chimps but not on children, when we have no reason to think the suffering would be less for the chimps – and when we know that no other differences are relevant.

Replies to this reasoning rely either on uncovering some morally relevant differences between the tested animals and humans or on justifying speciesism. The replies raise their own puzzles.

There are, of course, differences: children have the potential for considerably more enriched lives than chimps, monkeys and many other animals. That is no doubt true; but why should what is potentially the case carry such weight? Fertilized human eggs possess the potential to become people, yet we do not treat them as people and many, many people find abortions morally acceptable. We should also wonder whether it is really 'potential' that explains people's seemingly speciesist attitudes and, if it does explain them, whether their grounds are good. After all, the child could be one with such brain damage that she lacks any potential for further development.

Suppose a choice has to be made between saving a child or some non-human animal from temporary pain; pain which would cause no adverse long-term consequences for either. Most people would insist that protecting the child is the right thing to do. Yet, if the suffering is the same, what can justify that discrimination? And if we think that it is simply wrong to inflict suffering on a child, independently of overall beneficial consequences, why is this stance not also applied to non-human animals? Should not the relevant moral question be Jeremy Bentham's, namely, 'Can they suffer?' Well, that is a relevant question; but is it the only one?

Let us take the rejection of sexism, racism and speciesism further. One such suggested 'ism' is family-ism. Is family-ism also morally wrong? Is the preference that mothers have for their own children over others justified? How about friend-ism? Is a greater affection for our friends than for unknown people morally wrong? How about blonde-ism, good-looks-ism, music-lover-ism, nation-ism? These queer examples should remind us that we have numerous preferences, based on how we feel, and without them we should probably cease to be human. These examples should also remind us that we need to assess when preferences are justified and when they are not, if we are to have flourishing lives. A woman's preference for bearded men in her personal life should – it almost goes without saying – not be condemned (the author declares no interest here); but using that preference to judge, for example, which man told the truth in court should meet with rejection.

We are speciesist, and that in itself can paradoxically be used to show that we are not. Being speciesist, we feel far more distress at a child's suffering than a non-human animal's; so that itself generates a morally relevant difference in outcome.

*   *   *

A four-year-old child, chimp or rabbit also suffers from not knowing what is going on. From this we may conclude that there can be more reason not to conduct painful experiments on children, chimps or rabbits than on fully grown rational people. If the experiments are intended to benefit mankind, then at least the adults can grasp the value of that aim. Furthermore, performing tests on the young will, in all likelihood, damage their future adulthood or radically cut short their lives. That suggests that we should turn from children to the elderly. If testing is necessary, may there not be some people, nearing death, prepared to sacrifice themselves for others? At least their sufferings would be mitigated by the knowledge that it was all in a good cause.

In as far as we are repelled by such a suggestion (and, in view of my age and the topic, I do now declare some interest), perhaps we should cease to shut our eyes to the misuse of animals in experimentation. We should, of course, also cease to keep our eyes firmly closed to the many other harms visited upon many, many creatures, courtesy of various forms of horrendous farming methods.

 1. THE DANGERS OF HEALTH

 6. IN THE BEGINNING

 13. WOLVES, WHISTLES AND WOMEN

18

VOTE! VOTE! VOTE?

It's election day. You are a keen citizen of a democratic country, with a genuine choice between the parties and candidates. You know which party you want to win, so you are about to vote. But why bother?

'I want to come to the aid of my party and help it achieve success. By voting, I shall be doing my bit.'

That could be a good reason on some very exceptional occasions – but I bet this occasion is not one. I bet you live in a constituency in which you have no reason to think that the winning candidate will win by one or even just a few votes. Your vote, in such circumstances, will make no difference to the electoral outcome in your constituency. And even if it did, think how unlikely it is that whether your party gains power hangs on whether your preferred candidate is elected.

'Surely, my vote will make a teeny difference.'

Suppose you do vote. What difference would you have

made? If your candidate wins, then she'll win by one more vote than she would otherwise have done. If your candidate loses, then she'll lose by one fewer vote than otherwise.

'Well, that is a difference.'

But that is no difference with regard to who wins and who loses. And the difference it does make with regard to the size of the win is negligible. No one seriously thinks that a candidate who receives 29,547 votes would be so sensitive that she would be even happier had she received 29,548. No one seriously thinks that other voters will be more impressed by that extra one vote of support for your chosen candidate. It would be better, instead of voting, to do the ironing, stroke the cat or visit your lonely neighbour.

'But what if everyone thought like this?'

I guess your ironing would be done ever so quickly, your cat may get scared and your neighbour would be overwhelmed.

'Don't be silly. I mean, what if everyone decided not to vote?'

If everyone followed my reasoning, then arguably there would be undesirable consequences. But not everyone is going to follow the reasoning and think like this. So the 'What if everyone . . .?' test is redundant.

Why vote?

Some things that we do make only a very small difference — maybe a difference that we do not even notice, yet none the less a difference. If we join others who are also making only a very small difference, we may contribute to an overall big difference.

In times of water shortage, cutting down my water use will not be noticed, but it does contribute in a teeny way to the overall reduction. In a tug-of-war, perhaps my contribution to my team's tugging is puny and my team would still win without it, yet, by joining in, I am helping to secure the winning outcome; other members of the team need not tug quite so much.

Voting is different. Suppose that I do not vote. If my candidate loses by more than one vote, then had I cast my vote I should still not have helped her to win. If my candidate wins, then had I cast my vote I should not have made a difference to the fact that she won.

There are some reasons to vote that may stand up. You may feel it is your duty as a citizen. Mind you, it would be a curious duty, seeing that it is one without point. You may simply enjoy taking part or being seen to be casting your vote. In sceptical mode, allow me to add: feel free to take part in pointless exercises if you want; but would it not be more valuable to be seeing that lonely neighbour or getting the ironing done?

*   *   *

What if everyone thought that way? This refrain fascinates many people, including moral philosophers. The thought is that morality must generalize. We should not ask, 'What difference will it make if I do not vote — or if I walk on the grass or pick the flowers?' After all, no one will notice. The question to ask is, 'What difference would these actions make, were everyone to do the same?' It is a generalization test.

Let me give the generalization test a run for its money. Suppose that I really should take into account the consideration, 'What if everyone . . .?' What if what exactly? What if everyone who knew lots of other people were going to vote decided not to vote and do something more worthwhile? There is now a muddle over how to include or exclude knowledge that many people will in fact vote. Maybe I should ignore all facts about anybody else voting and act as if I am going to be the sole voter. Then my voting becomes highly, highly important, making the electoral outcome hang on my vote. Were that right, I should risk life and limb to vote. But that cannot be right – for I surely do not remotely rate my voting as *that* important.

We need to return to what is actually, in all likelihood, going to happen, rather than to the 'What if . . .?'s. What others do is sometimes affected by what I do. If I am the Prime Minister's partner, the latest pop group idol or a charismatic drug-crazed model, announcing that I cannot be bothered to vote may well influence others not to vote. Most of us lack such influence. So it looks like ironing, cat-stroking or neighbour-visiting should be our task at the next election.

Mind you, I strongly recommend that you do not spread this argument around.

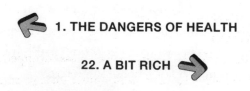

1. THE DANGERS OF HEALTH

22. A BIT RICH

19

WHERE AM I?

You know how it is. Tiring day at work, then journey, so slow, so slow, as homeward and boringly bound as ever. Long wait for crammed train, fiddling with coins (parking meter, you see) while rain it rains, so much rain it does. Arrive home – to rest, oh bliss, to drink, wind down. 'Mmm . . . things aren't that bad.' Stretch back on sofa – and transported you are . . . You're walking on air, blue skies above, entwined with lover(s); then, mysteriously racing, with tigers, tigers so stupendously striped, flying across oceans, landing back in the office but now making a speech, rapturous applause, telling bosses how hopeless, sacking them all. That lottery win's a boost, big boost to your ego, big boost to you. And it is all so real – so real, at the time, at the time; yet, of course . . .

It is all a dream.

You drift back to reality, wine glass dropped, stains on your shirt, ache in your neck (must change sofa) need

to get organized. There's bed yet to come, early start in the morning.

Now you're reading these words. It's the cold light of day. You're back on the train (I hope not driving the car). Or maybe you're holiday bound, airport lounge lounging, flight delayed, seat booking all wrong, but smiling at girl's smile opposite. Or perhaps, right now, you're thinking hard, drinking coffee so awful, wondering where this is going. Whatever, wherever, whoever, you know full well that now you're awake, wide awake now. This is no dream.

Yes, you surely can tell when you are truly awake. You well know that often, in dreams, you fail to realize that you are dreaming but you know, well enough too, from how everything looks, how everything feels, that right now and here, you are alert and awake, well awake at that. The things around you – the book, the pages, the coffee, your head – are no mere figments of dream-like life. No erotic encounters, no running naked through crowds. Yet, even if there were such events, you would be able to tell right now they were real. Or so it seems.

So, here you are, reading these words, in this all too orderly and mundane world, as undream-like as possible. And the next moment?

The alarm goes off; the cat licks your face; you have over-slept – and you realize you have been dreaming, dreaming about reading a book, a section on dreams.

How do you know you are not dreaming right now?

The dreaming puzzle was most famously presented by the seventeenth-century French philosopher, Descartes, the so-called 'father' of modern philosophy who made famous 'I think, therefore I am'. His answer to the question relied on his having already proved to his satisfaction that God exists; but it is difficult to believe that God's existence needs to be established before we can ever know that, on many occasions, we are not dreaming. Let us drop God. It is simply true that often we are utterly convinced – and indeed know – that we are not dreaming; but should we be convinced? What justifies our conviction? Do we ever know?

If asked to reflect on what makes us so sure that we are wide awake and not dreaming, we may point to the orderliness of our experiences, how they cohere with our memories and the constancy of the objects around us, an orderly world of home, family and friends. We are also aware of how vivid real life experiences are – how hard the wall is, how drenched we are from the rain, how painful the headache. Yet, any features we come up with, as being distinctive of being awake and not dreaming, may be challenged in two ways. Are they distinctive of being awake? And, even if they are, may we not merely be dreaming that our experiences right now have those features?

Suppose you think that the sheer orderliness of real experiences tells you that you are not dreaming. Is that true? Can you not have extremely orderly dream experiences? If that is so, then maybe this is one of those cases, of a very orderly – mundane – dream. But let us suppose that orderliness of experiences is the distinctive mark of being awake. This raises the question: how do we know that we are not merely dreaming that things are orderly? Whatever feature – call it 'F' – that we say our experiences must have in order not to be dreaming experiences, how can we ever be sure these experiences have F? How do we ever know that we are not merely dreaming they have F?

*   *   *

The mere possibility that, for all we know, we are dreaming is enough to make many people sceptical about what we claim to know. Descartes, and others, have tried to take things much further, supposing it is possible that we are being misled, not merely through dreaming, but perhaps courtesy of an evil demon intent on deceiving us as far as possible, or courtesy of mad scientists who have our brains in vats, feeding us experiences via electrodes. Film producers have taken such thoughts further, in virtual reality tales, such as the incomprehensible *The Matrix*.

The dreaming possibility gives a boost to philosophical sceptics, those who doubt whether people know what they reckon to know. Here is one simple sceptical argument:

(1) If I know that I am reading a book right now, then I know that I am not merely dreaming that I am reading.

(2) I do not know that I am not merely dreaming that I am reading.

(3) Therefore, I do not know that I am reading a book right now.

The conclusion (3) does indeed follow from premisses (1) and (2). The argument's form is *modus tollens*; we use it every day. 'If she's going to be late, she would have 'phoned. She's not 'phoned. Therefore she's not going to be late.' If we accept the premisses, we should accept the conclusion.

As the conclusion (3) follows from the premisses, if you are to reject the conclusion – that is, if you are to accept that you do know that you are reading this book – you are committed to at least one of the premisses being false. Premiss (2) seems unassailable: have we not already shown that we cannot know that we are not dreaming? Perhaps premiss (1) is at fault. Is it possible that, to know things, we do not need to know that we are not dreaming them? How on earth can that be? How can you know that you are reading this book and not merely dreaming that you are reading, if you cannot rule out that you may be merely dreaming that you are reading?

Even if you feel you can be sure about whether you are dreaming and can know, in some cases, that you are not – that is, even if you reject premiss (2) – the sceptical argument can be revised, replacing the dreaming possibility (as already noted) with that of a powerful demon or a mad scientist, out to deceive you as far as possible. If I know that I am reading a book, then must I not know that I am neither dreaming nor being deceived into thinking that I am reading when I am not, be it by a powerful demon or mad scientist stimulating my brain, so that I am caused to have these misleading experiences?

The possibility of a powerful deceiver – Descartes spoke of the possibility of an evil genius – perhaps gives us a deception too far. Suppose the deceiver is so good in her deceivings that we can never tell when we are being deceived: it still seems to us as if we go to work, read books, fall in love, take holidays, have a family, drink too much at parties, sing out of tune and so on. If any deceiver is that good at her deceptions, what becomes of the deceptions? They go up in a puff of smoke – or, better, they collapse, giving us the real world just as we know it – for is there any content to such universal deceptions? Deceptions that cannot, even in principle, be spotted by us are no deceptions at all. In contrast to such extreme seemingly deceptive possibilities, dreams often do take us in, yet we can eventually discover our mistakes. After all, we wake up – and sometimes we know it.

Here you are, indeed, in your waking state, knowing that you are reading this book and knowing full well that no morning alarm is about to go off in the next few seconds to wake you up . . .

Brr . . . Brrrr . . . Brr . . . Brrrr . . .

31. DON'T READ THIS NOTICE

32. MYSTERIES

 12. IT'S ALL RELATIVE

29. 'I AM A ROBOT'

20

OUT OF TIME

Some people live for the present. Others live in the past. Yet others live for the future. This is a little exaggerated, for we all need to have some concern for all three. At the very least, it is unclear quite what counts as 'the present'. (How long is the present?) Still, doubtless we know of people who tend to focus more on one temporal aspect of their lives than others. Here are some extremes.

Mr Past concentrates on what he has done: how he won that gold medal, built up his business and sported the largest yacht in the harbour – or (or even 'and') he may relive tragedies: the loss of his yacht, his business and his wife. What he is currently involved in, other than remembering, carries little weight. What he is going to do, next year, next month, even tomorrow, has scant impact. This attitude is most common among the elderly.

Miss Present lives for the present – for the moment. For her, no lingering on past successes and failures. Miss Present moves with the present. Projects for the future matter little. She just throws herself into whatever she is up to, in the here and now.

Ms Future focuses on the future. Like Miss Present, she ignores the past. Like Mr Past, she takes little notice of the present. Rather, she lives for what she will be doing, how well or badly things will be going – and so on. She takes great delight in the anticipation of her holiday next month; yet once on that holiday, she is dominated by bleak anticipation of its end.

Mr Past, Miss Present and Ms Future are extreme examples of people's different tendencies, yet if we consider happenings of like intensity and duration, we usually have far more direct concern for our present and future experiences than our past.

Consider this. You will suffer terrible pains resulting from a vital operation. I bet you would prefer them to be in the past, over and done with, rather than in the future. Or, some wonderful experiences are going to enthral you. I bet you would prefer that they are forthcoming, rather than that they be finished.

Why do we prefer pains to be in the past rather than the future?

Why prefer pleasures in the future to those in the past?

Usually, we think of ourselves as being the same selves over time. Memories sharpen and decay, characters develop, circumstances radically change, yet the cry goes up, 'But it is still me!' It is still me, however much my hair turns grey. If I am *me* and as much *me* throughout my life, ought not I to have the same amount of regard for me, for my existence, at any time? If I am the same self over time, it would seem most rational to have the same concern for past pains as for future ones – and to be as moved by past pleasures as future. Indeed, my *self* that existed ten years ago should carry as much weight for me as my self that will exist ten years hence – and, indeed, my self now. Ought I not to be concerned with my self, *out of time*, so to speak?

Some of our different attitudes to the past, present and future can, in part, be explained by intrusions to do with uncertainty. I am more stressed by the pain I am suffering now than the one I shall suffer next week because I may be able to prevent the latter or, for some reason or other, it may not happen. Were that the key to our different attitudes to past, present and future, we ought also to be more stressed about our past pains – they definitely happened – than future ones. Yet most of us prefer the visit to the dentist to be past than future. With pain, we want to be able to exclaim, 'Thank goodness that's over!'

Undoubtedly, we have temporal preferences. We prefer bad things to be over. We prefer good things to be forthcoming or happening now. Yet it is unclear whether anything can justify these preferences. Indeed, if I am the same self over time, it looks as if these temporal preferences are sheer prejudices – discriminations against my life to date and in favour of my life to come.

Some have argued that we should overcome these prejudices. On this view, if, through loss of memory and medical notes, it is currently unclear whether I suffered painful procedures yesterday or shall be undergoing them tomorrow, it is mistaken to hope that it turns out that the procedures took place yesterday. Either way is as bad for me. If you hear that your children or parents or lovers have been tortured and murdered in some far-off land, but then learn that there is some confusion about whether it has happened or is about to happen, should you not be equally distressed either way (assuming that there is no hope of avoiding the outcome for them)?

*   *   *

Relating the 'out of time' perspective with our living 'within time', where future happenings become present and then past, is tricky. Some argue that our temporal preferences do indeed display an inconsistency. Consider your experience of two pains of similar considerable intensity and duration, the only difference being that one occurred yesterday and is all over and the other will occur tomorrow. Are you not inconsistent in being far more concerned about the future pain than the past?

The answer is that the critic is forgetting that you were, no doubt, highly concerned about that past pain when it was yet to come, when it was then in the future and also when it was present and occurring. That past pain is less significant now than a similar future pain because when that past pain was future and then present, you paid as much attention to it as you are now doing to the forthcoming future pain. And the future pain that distresses you so much now – and even more when present – will eventually receive less concern from you, once in the past.

It looks as if we, with our temporal preferences, can avoid the charge of inconsistency, if we step back from where we are *now* in our lives; yet, of course, that does not touch the fact that we still do have the preferences, thinking our future experiences more important than similar past ones, from the standpoint of where we are now. It remains unclear whether those preferences are justified. Maybe nothing more can be said to defend them. Maybe they are indeed mere prejudices – or just how things are.

Our non-existence provides a striking example of our radically different temporal attitudes. Many people fear death, even when they believe that death is annihilation. Their lack of future existence is of great distress. Curiously, they rarely regret their lack of existence before birth, that is, their lack of prenatal existence. Is this also a prejudice? Or is Lucretius, from ancient Rome, right; that we should be as little concerned about being dead as about the time before we were born?

If prenatal non-existence is on a par with being dead, then – pessimist that I am – I wonder whether the distress we feel at the loss of our life at death should not also darken our feelings about the lack of life before birth. Should we be troubled by what we missed out on before we were born? Are we born too late? Do we die too early?

 8. WILL YOU STILL LOVE ME TOMORROW?

28. TENSIONS IN TENSE →

21

SAINTS, SINNERS AND SUICIDE BOMBERS

Allow me to introduce you to Sophie and Safia, two splendid and thoughtful young women. Sophie is Christian; Safia is Muslim.

Sophie was brought up in a Christian home, underwent no serious youthful rebellion and became more and more personally devoted to the teachings of Jesus Christ. She worships and prays. She speaks, sincerely, of listening to God. She relies on God concerning what is right and wrong, what she morally should and should not do. Sometimes she seeks guidance from others of her faith but they, in turn, rely on their communion with God or the communion of others with God, as described in the Bible. Sophie occasionally has religious experiences, which she describes in terms of 'seeing Christ'. She devotes considerable time to helping the underprivileged. She finds happiness in her religious life; we may say that she is blessed. Speaking somewhat loosely, Sophie is saintly.

All the above holds true of Safia, save she speaks of Allah instead of God, follows the teachings of Mohammed instead of Christ and relics on the Qur'an instead of the Bible. Safia too is, speaking even more loosely (given the Christian connotation), saintly.

Had Sophie and Safia been brought up differently – Sophie in Islam; Safia in Christianity – their religious beliefs, in all likelihood, would have been swapped. Imagine Sophie and Safia were identical twins, with the same genetic inheritance, whose mother died at their birth. Through chance, they ended up being nurtured in the different religions: Safia in Islam; Sophie in Christianity. Had they, as babies, been switched, Safia would have been nurtured in Christianity and Sophie in Islam.

It would seem that they are irrational in holding the religious beliefs they do, for they know that, had circumstances been different, they would have held to different religions. Whether or not the irrationality charge stands would appear of little consequence but for the vital fact that believers typically derive their moral beliefs (or think they do) from their religions. Given that different religions tell their believers different things about their morality's content and given that, had those believers been brought up in different religions, they would have adhered to different moralities, we may rightly ask:

How can religious believers rationally base their morality on religion?

We are lucky. Sophie and Safia understand the words of God and Allah, of Christ and Mohammed, of the Bible and Qur'an, respectively, in such a way that they seek peace, value kindness, perform charitable works and so on. But think how things could have been radically different. Safia might have listened and heard that she should be a martyr for Islam, become a suicide bomber and kill hundreds of innocent people. Sophie would be appalled at the thought – but is she in any better position? She also bases her morality on religion.

Had Sophie been in Safia's shoes (and maybe it is just chance that she is not), she too could be exposed to the injunction to become a suicide bomber. Wearing her Christian shoes centuries ago, Sophie could have been calling for the burning of witches, the slaughter of infidels and the forced conversion of Jews. Wearing her Christian shoes today and listening to the voice of God as understood by some, she could still be supporting bombing raids known to cause tremendous injuries to innocent people. If we start being more specific, we should note the different varieties of Christianity and of Islam; for example how, historically, Catholics tried to force the conversion of Protestants as well as Jews by various brutal methods. Reflect how, even today, many believers have it divinely revealed that homosexual acts are evil, contraception is wicked and a wife should obey her husband – while many other believers deny that God's commands are like that at all.

The most general expression of the danger being addressed in this puzzle is that if people base their moral beliefs – that is, their beliefs concerning how they should treat others and themselves – exclusively on an authority's voice, they run the risk of carrying out some highly immoral deeds and feeling themselves justified in performing them. There is no guarantee concerning what an authority commands. However, once people recognize that there are conceivable circumstances in which it would be wrong for them to obey the authority, they recognize they have some moral beliefs that are independent of that authority. Religious believers who reject religious voices telling them to be martyrs for the faith would be sinners in the eyes of the religion but may well be seen as secular saints, if their rejection means that they refuse to bomb innocent people. Indeed, it is the fact that many believers have moral beliefs not grounded in religious authority that often explains why they interpret their scriptures in such a way that the scriptures support those moral beliefs.

Believers may reply that even non-believers often base their morality on some authority – on the State, political creeds, parents' teachings or even teachings of philosophers. My reply is that submission to such authorities can be dangerous, unless the authorities are open to questioning, to reasoning and to respecting people and their feelings. Puzzles obviously persist concerning the basis of moral beliefs but, in general, there is significant agreement among people, in their everyday lives, about what is fundamentally right and wrong; an agreement that has no need of religious backing. That is not to say that non-believers never behave badly. It is not to deny that religious teaching has sometimes helped people to behave well. It is to insist that what is right and wrong cannot ultimately be understood in terms of what God or gods command, a point argued by Plato over two thousand years ago.

*   *   *

Are Sophie and Safia irrational in their religious beliefs in general? Consider some non-religious but factual beliefs about the world.

Almost certainly, you believe that, however far you travel on the Earth's surface, you will not fall off the edge. You almost certainly believe that the Earth orbits the Sun. But if you reflect, you will agree that, had you been born many centuries ago, you might well have thought that people could fall off the edge of the Earth and that the Earth certainly did not circle the Sun.

Even though you recognize that you would in all likelihood have held different beliefs about the world, had you been in radically different circumstances, that in no way undermines the beliefs that you hold today. This is because you recognize that, in those different circumstances many centuries ago, you lacked evidence that is now available. Where religious beliefs about God and the afterlife are concerned, based on scripture and revelations, is there, though, much scope for showing how one set of scriptures or revelations provides better evidence than another? It would seem not – and hence there is the irrationality of believing in one religion, while knowing that another would have been equally convincing.

Maybe this puzzle is what motivates certain disparate believers to speak of religious believers all really worshipping one and the same God. It motivates others to speak of 'leaps' (though rarely 'skips' or 'hops') of faith. Mind you, the leapers do not merely need faith to take the leap but also faith that their leap is the right leap.

Once the appeal to faith exists, any leap – however bizarre, dangerous or bad – would seem to be permitted.

24. LUCKY FOR SOME

32. MYSTERIES

3. SYMPATHY FOR THE DEVIL

22

A BIT RICH

Without a doubt, we live in a grossly unequal society. Numerous people, through no fault of their own, scrape by on low wages or no wages at all – and, if the latter, are at the whimsical mercies of State benefits. The poor have pretty dreadful living conditions and unhealthy lives, with little scope to improve themselves. Their children typically find themselves following suit. Okay, some of these poor are, I guess, scroungers but that does not mean we should ignore the many who are not. Society should be far more egalitarian; there should be far greater equality between people's standards of living and access to health and education – and far greater equality of opportunity. And then there's global poverty . . .

Polly – Polly Titian – is in full flow, interviewed in a pub near the Houses of Parliament. On her way out, she drops a pound coin into a beggar's hat and is then whisked off, in her chauffeur-driven Rolls, to her mansion in Hampstead; she needs to pick up her children, just returned from a well-known public school, before they all fly off to her yacht, moored near St Tropez. While on holiday, her children receive additional tuition – Polly wants them to do exceptionally well in their school examinations.

Polly – more accurately, Lady –Titian is an extreme case of wealth commenting on poverty but she is no different in kind from many politicians who argue that private schools should be abolished, yet send their children to private schools; from religious leaders who preach sermons, wringing their hands over the world's dispossessed, yet their preaching takes place in fine churches bedecked with great works of art; and no different from world leaders discussing global starvation at banquets with fine food and wine being served. She may, indeed, be no different from the many of us who agree that there are unjust inequalities and yet do little, so little.

We may explain Polly's position simply as hypocrisy. She knows what she ought to do – give away much, much more money – but she is selfish. Perhaps she is not weak-willed but ill-willed, even by her own lights. Let us not be satisfied with that response. Let us grant her some sincerity.

Can you sincerely want a more equal society while knowingly being wealthy?

'Champagne socialist' is the term that readily comes to mind but many non-socialist politicians are also committed to greater equality. It is plausible to believe that many – like

Polly — are sincere. She seems to recognize some obligation to help others: she makes small charitable donations and canvasses for electoral candidates who are for greater equality. She could, however, give much more, without dropping her standard of living at all. And she could give much, much, much more and still live comfortably, though without the chauffeur-driven Rolls, the yacht and the private education for her children.

Excuses for her behaviour are available. She may confess to being unable to part with money, even though she knows that she should. Alternatively, we may see her as irrational, engaged in self-deception over what she truly believes; but we are interested in whether she can be justified in declining to help more, despite her attachment to greater equality. In view of the small help that she does provide, she clearly is not a person who insists, 'It's nothing to do with me.' Can her stance be justified?

Whatever she gave, she would make little overall difference; society would still be radically divided between rich and poor. This thought does not carry weight: she makes small charitable donations, so why not bigger? It is true that if she is solely concerned about the relative poverty of the poor compared to the rich, then her donations, however large, would make little difference; but it is not true that they would make no radical difference to the welfare of *some* poor people. Improving the lot of the poor is typically the reason for seeking greater equality and Polly could achieve this for some, were she to give much more.

Maybe she believes that she has no obligation to help to put right injustices, such as inequalities, that are no fault of her own;

but it looks as if she feels she does have some sort of obligation in these matters. For example, she feels she ought to promote a more egalitarian society: witness her electoral work. It looks as if Polly is closing her eyes to what more she should be doing.

*   *   *

How Polly views her wealthy position is relevant. We are assuming that she acquired her wealth legally but she may, none the less, agree that she is not entitled to so much wealth, given the many poor around her. Perhaps she was lucky on the stock market or inherited her wealth. It is curious that many people who praise equality of opportunity and the importance of reaping benefits solely on the basis of merit also strongly condemn the taxation of inheritances — as if what people inherit should be fenced off from all questions of desert, merit and equality of opportunity.

Perhaps Polly's wealth derived from her entrepreneurial skills and business ventures. Even so, no doubt, she could have helped her employees much more than she did and, indeed, her business success occurred within the existing unjust society from which, doubtless, her business benefited.

There is a difference between thinking that a more egalitarian society should come about and thinking that you should help to bring it about personally. Were taxation increased and distribution of benefits changed, so that Polly's wealth was radically reduced, she may find that to be no problem at all. She would know that other wealthy people would be treated similarly. If, however, she were to reduce her wealth by her own charitable means, she would risk placing herself at a disadvantage to the wealthy who do not do likewise. She also would have the burden of deciding voluntarily to effect the reduction and, indeed, the burden of deciding which particular poor individuals to help – and can that be done without being unfair? Further, she may claim that, with her current wealth, she is able to influence government ministers and is, in fact, encouraging them to improve their policies on poverty. (She would, no doubt, hasten to add that her title no way results from the influence of her riches.) The strength of these claims is moot. Whether they are sufficiently strong to justify her lack of significant donations to the impoverished and dispossessed is highly doubtful.

Polly may insist that charitable help makes the poor dependent on charity and it would be better to be in a society where people received decent wages. Surely, though, having an improved standard of living through charity is better than no charity and no improved standard of living.

Can we square Lady Titian's wealth with her commitment to equality? Are not the attempted justifications for the concerned rich hanging on to their money all – dare we say? – a bit rich?

24. LUCKY FOR SOME

26. YOU'LL NEVER GET TO HEAVEN . . . ?

23

UNIQUELY WHO?

A strange thing happened the other day. I glanced at the man by the bar, just as he glanced at me (but this is no tale of gay love at

first sight). It struck us both how similar we looked – as if we were identical twins. We laughed, got talking and discovered the same interests. It transpired that we had been born in the same town. A little later, amazingly, it came out that we had the same birth date. Coincidences happen. We pursued matters further. Imagine my astonishment when he announced the exact time and place of his birth. Identical to mine! He named and described his parents. 'But they're my parents!' I said. He looked at me, his stare and my stare alike with incredulity. We found ourselves exploding with indignation, each exclaiming, 'But I'm Peter Cave. You're just pretending you're me.' We were embarrassed at making a public scene, so we got up and left. Bizarrely, we headed back to the same address. 'Ah,' I thought with some triumph, 'I have the only keys.' The triumph quickly subsided, as I saw him yanking out similar keys from his pocket . . .

The tale could be continued in various ways. The two sets of similar keys could open two similar houses containing two similar families – in exactly the same location? – or perhaps we returned to one and the same house, met one and the same family and so on. What it illustrates is that, however similar someone may be to me, surely he can never be me. Am I not unique? What is it that makes me *me* – and makes this me continue to be me?

Uniqueness applies to any object. There are many copies of this book; they could be very, very similar – the same creases, the same shaped coffee stains, in the same unread dusty state – yet, none the less, each copy is distinct because, even if all their features are the same, they are in different places or, if in the same place, in the same place at different times. The distinct copies consist of different sets of molecules – more colloquially, different lumps of physical stuff. The particular lump that makes up this copy cannot be both here and over there, at the same time.

So, what makes me *me* – and makes me continue to be me?

Is what makes me *me* the particular physical stuff out of which my body and brain are formed, just as this particular book is made from this set of molecules? If so, then maybe my continuation demands the continuation of the same physical stuff. Yet I can have heart, lung and liver transplants and still be me. New tissue can be injected into my brain and old tissue removed and yet I remain the same self, the same me. All my molecules are naturally replaced over the years.

Perhaps what makes me continue to be me is not being made out of literally the same physical stuff but there being a continuing, developing neural structure or organism, continuous in space and time. Or perhaps what is essential is not the same neural structure but the same continuing consciousness, with memories, desires and intentions developing, coming and going, with some appropriate degree of connectedness. After all, does it not make sense – at least, it seems to make sense – to conceive of waking up, with a different body and brain, as happened to the central character in Kafka's story, *Metamorphosis*? His disturbing tale opens with the words: 'As Gregor Samsa awoke one morning from uneasy dreams he found himself transformed in his bed into a gigantic insect. "What has happened to *me*?" he wondered.'

Some have conceived the possibility of another universe, a duplicate or 'identical twin' universe. Speaking loosely, in that universe there is another 'me', or so it seems, with the same neural structures as I have in this universe and with the same memories and desires; the same relationship to bar, house and keys. Yet that could not actually be *me*.

I am a particular item. Whatever stories are told of items having all the same properties and qualities and memories and relationships as I have, I cannot make sense of any of those items being me, apart from one – *me*. I make sense of myself continuing over time: I have a past and a future – and these past and future selves (as we may call them) must bear some special relationship to me now. Perhaps that relationship is, as some have suggested, one of psychological continuity, involving some connectedness. However, the psychological continuity answer needs to be able to handle cases of amnesia – and paramnesia, where people sincerely think they remember doing things which they have not done. If the psychological disruption is so great, perhaps that does indeed amount to the death of the person, of me. If all my memories have gone, all specific desires and plans and hopes, what is left of what can properly be identified as me?

Consider this: I am shortly to undergo some severe and prolonged pain. Perhaps an evil scientist is about to torture me. Being no masochist, I do not at all look forward to this future. If the scientist promises, 'I'll make things a little easier for you. I'll wipe your memories just before I begin the torture,' would my fear be reduced? My fear should surely be at least as great. I shall still be suffering the pain, even though I shall no longer know who I am. How would that help to stop its being me undergoing the pain? Aware of my distress, the scientist adds, 'After I wipe your memories, I'll give you a set of false memories. Maybe that will help.' Will it? I shall end up being mad as well as tortured. Surely, it will still be *me*, even though I shall remember nothing of my past and shall doubtless have a completely different personality.

The tale challenges the thought that what makes me me is the retention of psychological continuity. Suppose the new memories and character that I am given are those of someone else whose body and brain are receiving my psychological states. That does not seem to help me to conclude, 'This body, soon to be tortured, will no longer be mine, so I shall not feel a thing, for I shall then be inhabiting that other body.' Perhaps one simple truth is that what makes me me over time must, at a minimum, be one of either psychological continuity or physical continuity — but when these criteria come apart, we are unsure how to respond.

*   *   *

Maybe one day it will be possible to put me to sleep and transport me to different planets. Maybe all the physical and psychological information and neural structures that make me me – my complete specifications – are copied, leaving on Earth at most a lifeless blob, the lifelessness resulting from the copying procedures. The information is beamed to a distant planet called 'Distant Planet', where it is used to reconstitute me – a speedy form of interplanetary transport. True, the stuff is different on Distant Planet, but we have already seen that the actual physical stuff even on Earth changes, yet I may remain. I awake on Distant Planet, with everything relevant – same structured memory, desires, body, brain – intact. I say: 'Yes, it's me, Peter Cave; it wasn't at all painful. I wasn't really worried about its not working.'

At first sight, the above tale of scientific advance generates no problems, *if* the procedure in some way involves my body's destruction, down here on Earth. But suppose advanced procedures require no such destruction. I should awake on Earth and also on Distant Planet. How can I be in two places at once? Indeed, if I can be copied, so to speak, onto Distant Planet, I could be similarly copied onto multitudinous planets. The concept of my self demands that there be solely one, solely one *me*; yet everything about me seems open to replication – and hence more '*me*'s.

Suppose that I wake up on Earth, go to my favourite pub and sitting there is the Peter Cave – that 'me' – who, as a result of a beaming, should have been re-created on Distant Planet but due to a misdirected power surge is here on Earth and – having my memories and desires – has gone to his favourite pub and we get chatting . . .

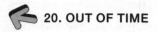 **20. OUT OF TIME**

29. 'I AM A ROBOT'

24

LUCKY FOR SOME

My apologies for another puzzling tale of violence. The puzzle occurs with all manner of actions which are open to moral blame or praise and which reap society's punishments or rewards. The excesses of violence can, paradoxically, bring puzzles to life. We start with Jack and Jill.

Jill took a liking to Jack's wealth and a disliking to Jack, so much so that she wanted to kill him, steal his money and escape to an isle of dreams. Jack was not keen on the idea and kept clear of Jill. Jill went hunting for her man. She found him at the top of a hill and tripped him up, knocking him unconscious, then drowned him in a bucket of water. It was horrendous behaviour. She was a deliberate killer. She was convicted of murder.

Had Jill failed to trip Jack or had the bucket been empty, then perhaps Jack would have survived. Jill would have been guilty of attempted murder, avoiding the longer sentence (or shorter, if a death sentence) associated with murder. Yet this difference in treatment resulted from events outside her control. She was as morally defective in both cases, though maybe practically more inept in the second. We may ask, by the way, why the law metes out different punishments when the moral wickedness is the same.

Whether people deserve moral praise or blame should not depend on accidents, luck or unluck, which are outside their control. The goodness (or otherwise) of our intentions is surely what matters morally. Suppose that when Jill met Jack at the hill's top, he happened to stumble, fell face down in the water and drowned – but Jill did nothing to save him. Is she not as morally culpable as in the first tale, when she drowned him? That raises a further puzzle of what morally relevant difference there is, if any, between killing and letting die, between the active and the passive.

Two more examples. You are sometimes careless when you drive. You fiddle with your lipstick, mobile telephone or car radio. You might have taken the odd drink too many. Few people treat you as being significantly morally blameworthy; yet if children run into the road and your reactions are slow and they are killed, are you not seriously blameworthy? In all likelihood, you would blame yourself for what you did. Yet the difference in extent of moral blame hangs solely on the children's running out, an event utterly outside your control.

Mr Miller is a family man, living in Britain, who has a limited choice of jobs available to him – security guard or gas fitter. He is easy to get on with, a man loved by his family and

friends. Consider a similar family man with similar characteristics: Herr Müller. He lived in Nazi Germany and the only jobs
available to him were working as camp guard or gas fitter in
Auschwitz-Birkenau. Through his job, he ended up at that camp
being involved in the killing of hundreds of thousands of innocent Poles, Russians and even more Jews. 'What a morally disreputable person! How could anyone have anything at all to do
with such horrendous evils!' Yet is it not circumstances – circumstances outside the control of both Miller and Müller –
that determine which of these two is deemed morally nice and
which morally nasty? Many of us are incredibly lucky not to
have been placed in circumstances where, in all likelihood, we
should find ourselves acting similarly to Herr Müller.

Should we be morally praised or blamed only for things within our control?

Immanuel Kant answered 'yes'. Writing around 225 years ago,
he insisted that a good will should shine like a jewel, independently of what it accomplishes or fails to accomplish. A bad will,
we may add, is like a black hole of evil, whether or not it draws
in others. Even if Jill fails to kill Jack, her will or intent marks
her as morally disreputable. Even if no child gets injured, we
remain morally reprehensible if we drive carelessly. Even
though Miller has a peaceful gentle life, if his character is such
that, in awful circumstances, he would allow himself to be
involved in horrendous killings, then he is as bad as Müller.

The puzzle is that, if we shield moral assessment from anything to do with what lies outside our control, we are in danger of losing morality completely. We spoke of Miller and Müller's characters. Did they have any control over what characters they would have – whether they would be courageous or weak-willed, principled or fickle, good at assessing moral responsibilities or not?

Consider Jasmin, a highly impressionable young woman who is swept along by what her family and close friends do. Consider what happens to Jasmin, depending on which community she lives within. In a Western, liberally educated setting, in a family of non-believers, she is pretty likely to be tolerant, easy-going, valuing individuality and the democratic vote. But bring her up reciting the Qur'an every day, being told by certain teachers that she must sacrifice her life to further Mohammed's word and she may become highly intolerant, even turning to terrorism. It is worth pointing out that, as well as the Christian and other religious faiths, non-religious movements have encouraged the killing of innocents. The point is not to engage in the debate of when, if ever, such killings are justified. The point is that, if our moral worth must not depend on accidents outside our control, what is left?

*　　　*　　　*

In the moral world, we muddle through, sometimes allowing outside factors to excuse us for what we do and sometimes not. But should we? Some try to escape the muddle by examining what should be counted as being within our control. Individuals are told to pull themselves together and be brave. If they fail, they reap the moral condemnation of being cowardly. But whether they can pull themselves together would seem to depend on characteristics over which, ultimately, they are powerless. It may also depend on the luck of having people around them, telling them to pull themselves together.

In the legal world, we also muddle through. The sentences meted out to criminals can be reduced, or even quashed, if the defence lawyers manage successfully to argue that the criminal was mentally disturbed and that his actions were not really under his command, and so not really *his* actions at all. Yet being mentally undisturbed does not count as a mitigating factor.

A thief argued that he was terribly sorry but he could not help what he did, given his bad upbringing; hence, he should not be held responsible for his thievery. The judge replied that she too was terribly sorry but, given her own upbringing, she could not help but give him a long sentence.

 10. MARY, MARY, QUITE CONTRARY

 21. SAINTS, SINNERS AND SUICIDE BOMBERS

 23. UNIQUELY WHO?

25

'I SHOT THE SHERIFF'

Sheriff has been seriously wounded while trying to stop Bandit's raid on a remote ranch. He clings on to his faithful horse, which gallops him back to Little Rock (as faithful horses do); Bandit returns to the Bandit family in its mountain hide-away. Bandit boasts, 'I shot the sheriff,' shows off his ill-gotten gains and initiates sustained celebrations. Back in Little Rock, beloved Sheriff is tended by the Little Rock doc, while a lynch mob sets off in search of Bandit. Sheriff, man of the law, makes clear his opposition to any lynching – 'I'm only shot, not killed. Bring Bandit back alive!' – but he (rightly) fears the worse, both for Bandit and for respect towards the law.

Celebrations in the hideaway are so noisy and drunken that Mob, after a few days' riding, has little difficulty in finding the required bandit. Bandit is lynched. Mob returns to Little Rock, where the Little Rock doc still struggles to keep Sheriff alive. Doc does his best – but his best is not good enough (no doubt

aided by Doc's propensity for gin). A few weeks later, Sheriff dies from his wounds, still displeased by the lynching. It is worth noting that we already have a puzzle: given his gin-soaked ineptness, should the doctor be held directly responsible for Sheriff's death rather than Bandit? Let us place that matter to one side by making Doc a highly competent teetotal doctor. Bandit undoubtedly killed Sheriff; he died of the wounds from Bandit's gunshots.

When Bandit killed him may be thought to be baffling. Did he kill him when he shot him? That is highly implausible: Sheriff remained alive for weeks after the shooting and so there is no way he could have been killed by the shooting, *at the time of the shooting*, while yet going on living afterwards. Did Bandit kill him at the point when he died? That too seems implausible, for when Sheriff died, Bandit had been dead for a few weeks, lynched by Mob. How could a dead man, in these circumstances, kill? It is not as if Bandit's corpse swung round in the noose and gave Sheriff a fatal blow.

Where the killing took place may also be thought baffling. The shooting occurred at the ranch but Sheriff was never dead at the ranch. He died in Little Rock, yet Bandit never went into Little Rock. When Sheriff eventually died there, Bandit was but a corpse in a remote mountain range.

When and where does a killing take place?

This is no mere academic question: the law needs to decide about such matters. Assuming Bandit acted intentionally (and that various other conditions were met), Sheriff's killing is a murder but where and when did the murder take place? The location may be highly relevant because where a law is broken usually determines the punishment: in some places murderers receive short so-called 'life' sentences (maybe ten years), yet elsewhere they meet with the death penalty (an extremely shortened life sentence). The time a crime occurred can also be highly relevant, for which punishment is meted out hangs on the law at the time of the offence and the age of the offender.

The right way of looking at this may be simply to remember that the law needs to decide about such matters. For practical reasons, we do just need to make decisions. It would be a mistake to think that, by investigating the world, we can rightly conclude that the murder occurred at precisely this point or that point. Perhaps the underlying mistake is to think that there must be precision when there is none.

The facts may be, for example, that a murder occurred in Virginia and in 1892 — but Virginia, and indeed 1892, are pretty big. No doubt we can be more precise about the murder but we should not assume that, in principle, we are always able to pinpoint a murder's time and location to a very high degree of specificity. A murder need not be space-time specific or have a precise location, akin to that of when and where a small alarm first went off.

Returning to Sheriff and Bandit, the correct description is as given in the tale. There was a shooting; it was fatal because some weeks later, in a different place, Sheriff died from his wounds. Legislators need to make decisions as to which laws should apply and, for the sake of justice, they need to ensure consistency. That is all that can be said.

*   *   *

Or perhaps we can say more. There arc many areas in life where the need to make decisions about which rules, regulations or laws should apply has not yet arisen. Imagine a football game in which a player kicks the ball a moment before being shot dead; a few seconds later, the ball ends up in the net. A dead player scored. Do the rules permit that? Not being a footballer, I do not know, but there is no difficulty in football games occurring without specific rules to cover that unusual eventuality. Or imagine a chess player makes a move, has a heart attack and immediately dies; his opponent studies the board, slowly realizes his position is impossible and resigns. The deceased player won — after his demise? Is that allowed?

We should not be surprised that what is true of people can start to apply after their death. Someone who has deliberately taken a poison, one which works slowly, only becomes a successful suicide when dead, not when she took the poison — but there is no clear answer, in such a case, as to when she committed suicide. Bandit became the murderer of Sheriff after his, Bandit's, death but that should no more strike us as curious than the fact that a woman in New York can become a widow because something happens in Shanghai — the death of her husband — and can become a grandmother because her daughter gives birth thousands of miles away in London. To think that, for there to be such truths, there must be changes in the New York woman over and above the changes in Shanghai and London is a mistake that (arguably) Leibniz made.

Usually what we do involves causal chains. She poured the petrol and threw a lighted match, which ignited the petrol and set fire to the curtains, which caused the wood panelling to catch light which caused . . . and so on. Small wonder that whether she burnt the house down depends on what happened some time after the initial pouring and match throwing.

Developments in the preservation of frozen human sperm, eggs and embryos may well raise more questions — in this area, about when and where fathering and mothering take place.

Oscar's sperm and Olivia's eggs were taken in 2007; fertilization occurred in 2009; the embryo was implanted in a womb in 2011 and the child was born in 2012. When did Oscar father, and Olivia mother, the child? Maybe they both died just before the sperm and eggs were collected; maybe they died in 2008 or 2010 and at different times. Some men have said, with a twinkle in their eyes, that they are not *knowingly* fathers. Give it time and both men and women may sometimes be able to say this – and be able, metaphorically, to say it even from the grave.

The grave may be a 'fine and silent place' but no longer does it rescue us from becoming parents.

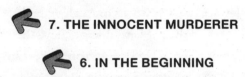

7. THE INNOCENT MURDERER

6. IN THE BEGINNING

28. TENSIONS IN TENSE

26

YOU'LL NEVER GET TO HEAVEN . . .?

Millions of people believe in a traditional single God, be it the God of the Jews, of the Christians or Allah of the Muslims; and they want to go to heaven. Many, many believe that the way to achieve heaven is to obey God's commands. Perhaps this is to misunderstand the religious texts but our puzzle arises from what many, many religious people believe, whether or not the belief is true. One godly command is a moral one – that we should help others – and, most importantly, that we should help others for their sake rather than as a means of gaining something for ourselves, such as advancing entry into heaven.

The puzzle is that this would seem to leave atheists and agnostics in a better position, with regard to heaven-entry through moral action, than reflective believers in God. Contrast Althea, an atheist, with Godfrey, a god-intoxicated, firmly committed, believer. Althea possesses a strong sense of moral duty; she values improving the lives of others and seeks no reward in return. She is a good person. As an atheist, she certainly is not motivated by desire for, or hope of, heavenly eternal life, yet she would pass any moral test for heavenly entry. (There may be other tests she would fail.)

What of Godfrey? He believes that, if he acts morally, he will reap the benefits of passing the moral test at heaven's gate. We need to break Godfrey down, so to speak, into two versions: a simple and a complex.

Simple Godfrey was a pretty immoral character before he came to believe in God and grasp what God commanded. He began to understand that he must help others, for their own sake, as a necessary condition for his reaching the desired heavenly end. 'But,' he reasoned, 'there is then no point in my helping others, because what is leading me to do this is my desire for heaven (or fear of hell) and that makes the whole point . . . er . . . pointless. To pass the heaven test, I need to act morally, without any self-interested motivation, yet I am considering what is best for me to do to pass the heaven test and improve my chances of a heavenly afterlife. That makes anything I do, as a result of such reflections, motivated by self-interest. My simple aim of achieving heaven seems, paradoxically, to prevent my doing what is required for heaven.'

Complex Godfrey, in contrast, was already genuinely concerned for others, for their sake not his. He was akin to Althea, in that respect. Since learning that this behaviour apparently helps to secure heavenly entry, he is vexed. He wants to get to heaven and he knows that his moral behaviour aids him in this quest, so maybe his motivation in helping others is no longer pure but is tarnished by self-interest. Maybe his motivation is now a complex and unhappy mixture: what he formerly sought for its own sake, he now seeks, or also seeks, for his own benefit; for the sake of passing through heaven's gate.

Is it easier for atheists to get to heaven than for believers?

There are, no doubt, some entrance conditions to heaven, in addition to those concerning moral motivation (assuming there is sense in the idea of entrance conditions). These conditions may well affect atheists and believers differently. On the one hand, atheists may have an even greater chance of heaven than believers if, for example, God sets lower standards on behaviour for those unaware of his laws than for those who are aware. On the other hand, believers may be better off than atheists because, presumably, conditions for heavenly entry may also include belief in God, worship of God and even certain rituals – all, by the way, rather unfair conditions for atheists who genuinely cannot feel justified in believing in God. One further condition could be that of wittingly obeying God's commands, which raises another motivational puzzle akin to the one already presented: God's commands include our treating others well for their sake – and probably not because God has so commanded.

Being motivated by God's commands and being motivated by a heavenly afterlife need not contaminate being motivated by the plight of others. People can be genuinely motivated to help others for their own sake and be genuinely motivated to do what is required to reach heaven, yet, because they are unaware of the link between the two, there is no puzzle: they simply do not realize that helping others is a means of increasing heavenly chances. Simple Godfrey may be able to take this path of ignorance. He could set about helping people, albeit with the wrong motives yet, over time, come genuinely to be helping them for their sake because he forgets the link with heavenly entry and how he got started on the path.

More likely, Simple Godfrey would find himself eventually becoming Complex. He ends up helping others – and for the right reason as far as he can tell – but he worries about how this ties in with his behaviour apparently also helping him to get where he wants: heaven. Is there a genuine problem here?

You may be motivated to do X, knowing that X brings about Y, yet not be motivated by Y. That is easily seen when Y is undesirable: you are motivated to visit friends in Zürich, yet know that they will lead you into extravagances and exhaustions, which certainly do not motivate you. But what if the further known outcomes are desirable? For example, in Zürich, your friends will take you to its famous opera house, something that you prize. Is that also part of your motivation? By way of finding the answer, you could consider whether you would still be Zürich bound even if the opera were closed. If you would, that suggests that seeing your friends is at least your primary motivation. Does this help vexatious Complex Godfrey?

For Complex Godfrey to have the right motivation, we need him to help others, even without the consequence of the increased likelihood of heaven – even if, indeed, there were no God. As Godfrey is a seriously committed religious believer, can he make sense of such a possibility: of there being no God; of not wanting to go to heaven? If he is unable to make sense of it, how can he assess what he would still do in, for him, such a senseless world?

The answer perhaps is that no requirement exists for him to be able to carry out the 'Would I still?' test, just that it be possible for someone to carry it out about him. Step forth the atheist – now, arguably (albeit paradoxically) again in a better position than a believer to evaluate the believer's true motivation.

*   *   *

When told that the first shall be last, we should be at sea for, once the first are last, then, being no longer first, presumably the new 'firsts' should be last – and so on. 'Help others, but be not motivated by this command' also has something of the marine queasiness about it. Motivations do not generate puzzles solely for the religious. Many people want happiness, yet believe the best way of securing happiness is by not directly seeking it; so must they somehow conceal their happiness goal from themselves? John Stuart Mill, who thought that happiness is most likely to be secured if not consciously sought day by day, also argued that, although society's best outcome is the utilitarian one (the greatest happiness of the greatest number), it does not follow that we should be motivated by that. John Austin, a friend of Mill, notes that, although utilitarians approve of love because it accords with utilitarianism, they are far from contending that a lover should kiss his mistress with an eye to the common welfare, to the overall resultant happiness. Were our relationships dominated by such utilitarian calculations, happiness would assuredly not result.

Some utilitarians have also argued that the greatest happiness would be achieved by people in general *not* believing in utilitarianism but believing instead that there are some moral rules that should never be broken, whatever the outcome. If these utilitarians are right then, as intimated in the voting paradox discussion and elsewhere, there are some things that should be kept secret from the public at large – including the fact that some things should be kept secret.

Shh . . . shh . . .

 16. JUST HELPING OURSELVES

 18. VOTE! VOTE! VOTE?

 1. THE DANGERS OF HEALTH

 3. SYMPATHY FOR THE DEVIL

27

CHICKEN! CHICKEN! CHICKEN!

'Chicken' is a game played by the rough and tough; well, only the rough and tough can face playing this version. Our players are two macho young men, Angelo and Berto, motorcyclists, bare chests bedecked with gold chains; lovers of revs and roar; of leather, rubber and heat; men out to impress the chicks; men who cannot face losing face; mean macho men of mean machines.

The game is simple. From opposite ends of a long straight road, they accelerate towards each other, chests puffed out with confidence and conceit, hair streaming in the wind. (Helmets? Not for true macho men!) They come at each other fast, driving along the central white line, getting closer and closer to a head-on crash. The one who veers away into the correct lane first (left, in Britain) is 'chicken' – fear, or good sense, finally taking over. The worse games are those in which the chicken chickens out pretty early on, quite a few seconds before a possible crash. We shall ignore degrees of chicken-icity.

The best outcome for Angelo is the one in which Berto veers away while he, Angelo, roars on, making Berto the chicken and Angelo the hero, receiving appropriate rewards from the chicks. The worse outcome for Angelo is that he chickens out, leaving Berto the road. The second best outcome (for both) is that they veer away at the same time into their respective lanes, just before it is too late. Some may argue this leaves them both chickens but wiser counsel is that they both merit congratulations for their nerve, judgement and final good sense. The only remaining possible outcome is a stupendous crash – not exactly good for either but, in their macho world, not as bad as being the sole chicken.

Apart from the risk of that stupendous crash, what is the

problem? 'Rationality' is, paradoxically, the answer. Yes, we are, counter-intuitively it is true, making Angelo and Berto rational individuals, as far as that is possible for people who play this game.

Angelo reasons: 'Either Berto will chicken out or he won't. If I keep my nerve, he might well chicken out before me; if he does, I win. But suppose Berto is not chicken: then for me to chicken out would be the worse outcome for me; remember, my machismo leads me to prefer a crash to such dishonour. So, whatever Berto ends up doing, I should hold my nerve, drive on, no veering.'

Berto reasons likewise. Reason tells both of them not to veer away, leading them to their worse but one alternative — and to the hospital (or the mortuary). There is a better option for both: to veer away just before crashing. Why not do that? Because if Angelo reckons that is what Berto will do, he may as well drive on and win; but Berto reasons likewise, if thinking that Angelo will veer away.

What if they secretly promise each other that they will both veer just in time? If Angelo is sure Berto will keep his promise, why should Angelo keep his? Macho men are ashamed of chickening but not of lying. Of course, Angelo would be aware that Berto would also be thinking that he, Berto, need not keep his word. Once again, a crash looks inevitable, if the players are rational.

Is it ever rational to co-operate?

This is no silly game. Imagine Andorra and Bermuda are nations at loggerheads in an arms' race, in possession of the same conventional weaponry. Andorra wants to be militarily stronger than Bermuda: it plans to develop nuclear weapons. For Andorra, the best outcome is Andorra with such weapons and Bermuda without. That is the worst option for Bermuda; it wants just the reverse. The second-best option for both is for neither to develop nuclear weapons: nuclear weapons are costly and, if they both end up with them, nothing of value is achieved. Both having nuclear weapons is a worse option than neither having nuclear weapons. Co-operation is in their mutual interests; they should agree not to develop nuclear weapons. But why should either party honour such an agreement? From Andorra's perspective, if Bermuda sticks to the agreement, Andorra would be better off secretly breaking the agreement, developing nuclear weapons and achieving its desired superior position. And if Bermuda secretly does not stick to the agreement, then Andorra needs all the more to be breaking the agreement and going nuclear.

These are examples of the prisoner's dilemma, so-called because it is typically put forward in terms of two prisoners. We shall call them Al and Belle. Al and Belle are being interviewed separately by the police, who are seeking confessions to their joint crime. Al and Belle do not know what the other will say, yet each must decide whether to confess. If neither confesses, their sentence will be a couple of years in prison: if one confesses and the other stays silent, the confessor is released and the silent one will receive ten years; if they both confess, they get five years each. Without trust, they will both confess and end up with five years each in prison – just as, without trust, the motorcyclists end up crashing and the nations pointlessly developing nuclear weaponry.

| | | **B** | |
		Keeps central Goes nuclear *Confesses*	**Veers away** No nuclear *Stays silent*
A	**Keeps central** Goes nuclear *Confesses*	**Crash** Futile expense *Five years prison*	BEST FOR A WORST FOR B
	Veers away No nuclear *Stays silent*	WORST FOR A BEST FOR B	SENSIBLE SECOND BEST FOR BOTH

A = **Angelo**/Andorra/*Al*; **B** = **Berto**/Bermuda/*Belle*

The dilemma is how to gain the mutual advantages of co-operating, if – as it seems – such co-operation involves the risk of the other party not co-operating. Is that risk a genuine risk? Reasoning through the alternatives leads us to do something that *seems* to be in our own best interests, whatever the other party does, yet it fails to give us the best result.

*   *   *

These are theoretical examples, in which the players seek to be rational by way of seeking their individual best outcomes rather than the mutual best outcome. However, what we do is determined by factors other than such rationality. We get to know people and learn how they react in a variety of circumstances. As a result, we often have reasons to think that others are trustworthy and likely to act co-operatively. Importantly, we are often aware that if we fail to co-operate or break our promise, it is less likely we shall receive co-operation from others when we need it. The likelihood of repeated prisoner's dilemmas gives a boost to our selecting the co-operative choice, the sensible second-best choice, in the examples.

Reasoning about repeated cases, however, does not provide a watertight solution to such dilemmas. Sometimes we know that no future cases will arise and even when we know there will be an indeterminate number of future cases, we are still taking a risk in a decision to co-operate and trust the others involved. Many of us, though, do find ourselves taking co-operative risks. Doing so is often to our benefit, even if it is irrational from the perspective of a single self-interested individual – and it at least avoids the head-on crash towards which Angelo and Berto, the rational bikers, are heading.

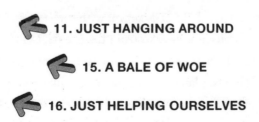

11. JUST HANGING AROUND

15. A BALE OF WOE

16. JUST HELPING OURSELVES

28

TENSIONS IN TENSE

While you read these words, the Earth orbits the Sun. A long time before your reading of these words, various rock formations changed and continents drifted, occurrences with long names with which only geologists are familiar. Numerous eclipses, comets trailing and stars a-shooting will occur some time after your reading, details of which only astronomers are competent to predict. In summary, things *are* happening, *have* happened and *will* happen. Saying the same thing, but differently: many events are in the present; many in the past; and many the future.

Now — and we should be careful with such (un)timely terms — delete all conscious beings from the events. Let us have only non-conscious happenings: geological changes and movements of clouds, planets, comets and the like. Even (and happily) ignoring the complexities of relativity theory, there are puzzles. When no conscious observers exist, are some of those events still in the present? Are some past? Some future? Or, for anything to be in the present, past or future, must it, at least, be related to individuals having experiences, having a viewpoint?

Presumably, we should insist that, even without conscious beings, events certainly occur. And if events occur, changes occur. Some states and events come after other states and events; those which went before. In a universe without conscious beings, there would still be temporal relationships of 'before' and 'after'. But would there be any temporal properties of 'present', 'past' and 'future'? Would there be tenses? Would there be truths to the effect that things had happened; things are happening; and things will happen?

Perhaps we are inclined to say 'no'. The existence of a past, present and future requires a point of view, a view from where things are, indeed, past, present and future. If there are no conscious beings, there is no viewpoint; there are just events in a 'before and after' sequence.

Were we inclined to agree that, at the very least, we need a viewpoint for there to be any sense in the idea of events being past, present or future, we may become even more suspicious of 'past', 'present' and 'future' concepts. What is this talk of 'viewpoint'? Perhaps all that can be rightly meant is that some events are before, some after and some simultaneous with any given viewing event. If the viewers are speakers, then when they say that certain geological changes occurred in the past, all they are really saying is that those changes occurred *before* their current utterances. The eclipses and other changes that will occur – future eclipses and other future changes – are examples of happenings *after* their utterances. Further, some of the Earth's movements are occurring at the same time as their utterances – 'occurrences now' or 'occurrences in the present'.

There is a metaphysical question here. Are 'past', 'present' and 'future' nothing more than our ways of referring to events that are before, simultaneous with or after someone doing the referring? More simply:

Is talk using tenses just talk about what is before, after or simultaneous with the talk?

When we speak of 'talk' we are, of course, alluding to any event – a thought, a hope, a speech – whose content involves reference to what is taken to be past, present or future. Many philosophers have argued that 'past, present and future' talk (and this applies to tensed talk) is simply reducible to 'before, after and simultaneous with' talk, hereafter referred to as 'before and after'. 'Past, present and future' gives us nothing more than that. Can this be right?

If talk of the present or 'now' is merely a matter of saying that some events are simultaneous with this talking, are we not missing the fact that these events simultaneous with this talking are indeed *now* – and not past or future? There are more problems: events, occurrences, happenings – events causing other events – all involve change. Does an understanding of time purely in terms of 'before and after' capture change?

Although, in recent years, there has been some publicity for Wittgenstein's poker – a controversy concerning whether, at a 1940s Cambridge Moral Sciences meeting, Wittgenstein, brandishing a poker, threatened Karl Popper – there is another, arguably more significant, Cambridge poker. It occurs in an example used by McTaggart, a few decades before the Wittgensteinian controversy.

Consider a poker: coloured red at one end and black at the other. Although it possesses these different colours, the possession does not carry with it the idea of its *changing* colour, merely that it *has* different colours. Similarly, that the death of Plato occurred *after* that of Socrates and *before* your reading of these words fails to capture the change we have in mind, when we speak of Plato's death once having been in the future but now being well in the past.

Consider now a black poker placed in a fire: it becomes red at one end because of the heat; still black and cold at the other. As the heat spreads, the black cold end will also turn to red hot – a change through time. The change is that the end that presently *is* cold and black, *will* become hot and red and, once hot and red, it is then true that it *was* cold and black.

Events involve change and change involves an item's properties – such as being hot and red – being future, then present, then past. If that is so, what account can we give of events changing from possessing the property of being in the future to possessing the property of being present and then past? A natural way of understanding such talk is, as said, in terms of how the events stand in relation to the speaker. But that, seemingly, involves merely the 'before and after' relation – and that fails to carry any implication of temporal change.

Your reading of these words is after certain historic geological changes; timelessly and always after those changes. You are reading these words before the Sun burns out; timelessly and always before that burning event. Events do not change their position in the 'before and after' series; so it is difficult to see how that series can be all there is to talk of past, present and future – for events do change their status as being past, present or future.

* * *

Time, and the idea of time, present many such troubles. McTaggart settled for time being an illusion. He argued that time does indeed essentially involve past, present and future, yet he, McTaggart, could make sense only of events standing in the 'before and after' relation.

To say that time is an illusion immediately generates its own paradox. Even illusions seem to involve time; even if it is an illusion that the tortoise is moving, none the less there seem to be changes in that illusion, such that some experiences, as if the tortoise were at point A, are in the past, while at present the tortoise seems to be at point B.

Here is another thought. I call it the 'paradox of time-taking'. It is quite common to accept that, one way or another, what is happening now in the universe (at least at the level of planets and trees and clouds) has been caused by, and is in some way explained by, what happened in the universe just before. The thought is that the state and events of the universe a little earlier are sufficient – enough – to bring about the state and events of the universe now. Were they not sufficient, we should need to postulate something else to explain why the things that are happening now are, indeed, happening now. So, we have the picture of the universe in state C being sufficient to bring about the universe in state E. If that is so, there is a puzzle about why it takes time (and the particular time it takes) for E to come about, once C is present. Why is E not instantaneous with C? If there is a time lag, then it shows that something else must have been required, as well as C, to bring about E.

The puzzle that results from the above reasoning is as follows. We are inclined to think of the states and events of the universe as standing in causal chains, over time. Yet this simply cannot be so – for such a chain would have to be an instantaneous 'everything happening all at once'. A big bang, bigger, indeed, than any big bang dreamt of by the scientists.

That's philosophy for you! And we didn't even leave our armchairs.

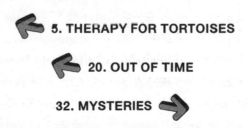

← 5. THERAPY FOR TORTOISES

← 20. OUT OF TIME

32. MYSTERIES →

29

'I AM A ROBOT'

'I am a robot – a mechanical woman, a mechanical doll indeed. Well, so I have just been told. I thought I was like everyone else – a person, with thoughts and imagination, intentions and memories, pains and pleasures – but apparently this is not so. Certain philosophers have explained that there is a huge difference between people and me. People have private experiences. I do not. How can this be? As far as I can tell, I differ in no crucial way at all.

'"Ah, yes, as far as you can tell," reply silver-tongued philosophers, "but you have been cunningly created, to appear like a person; yet you are no person at all."

'Well, I am made from biological material. My mechanism does not consist of crude wheels and pulleys but of electro-chemical activity in a neural system, just as in people's. I am humanly shaped – rather desirably so, if I may modestly add. I have brain and heart and womanly pulsations – laughs and talks

and coquettish walks. Tears fall from my eyes when onions I peel, when I lose at the races and when I see my lover(s) dancing too closely to others. My voice is unsteady after a little red wine – how I do prefer champagne! – and my heart skips when some handsome gigolo meets my gaze.

'That is how it all seems to me but, apparently, I have no conscious life, no experiences, no true "seeming to me" at all, if "seeming to me" involves conscious experiences. I use the right words for consciousness, experiences and the like; I react as people typically react – but all this, I am told, is not because of any awareness or consciousness or feeling on my part.

'Tread on my toe – and I jerk my foot away, wince and cry "Ouch!" Yet, so they say, I experience no private painful sensations. Everything that goes on inside me is open to scientists observing my neural and other bodily changes. And however deep within me they peer, they spot no thoughts, no images, no pains, no pleasures. You, reader(s), by contrast, have private sensations and thoughts, such consciousness that I, apparently, lack. Although I can, as well as any regular person, discriminate between hot and cold, light and dark and loud and soft (and act accordingly), I am, it seems, no better than a complex thermostat, light sensor and sound apparatus rolled into one – and certainly they lack feelings of heat, sensations of sight and experiences of sound.

'I break down at this news. I am terribly hurt by what these philosophers say about me. My distress proves nothing at all, for – to them – it cannot be a distress that involves my having sensations. They congratulate themselves on how much like a real person I am.'

Is there more to *you* than your behaviour, body and brain?

Are your experiences different from the physical things happening within you?

What are we to make of Miss Doll, who spoke so movingly? Might someone, who speaks and reacts almost exactly as we do, be without conscious experience?

Some philosophers – and even some sensible people – believe such robots to be logically possible. They argue that conscious experiences are over and above – are different from – what goes on inside brains and bodies and the movements that get done or are likely to be done. Therefore, they add, there is no contradiction in there being an individual such as Miss Doll who is, in all relevant respects, like us, except that she ('it'?) lacks conscious experiences. She performs as we all do but when she and we are reading these words, we have visual experiences, whereas she has none. Such creatures, who seem like us yet who lack experiences, are called by some philosophers, somewhat misleadingly, 'zombies'.

Other philosophers argue that, as Miss Doll is the same physically as we are and acts in the same ways as we act or are likely to act (apart from her recent discovery of seemingly being a robot), she is, indeed, a person with experiences – and it is sheer nonsense for her, or us, to believe otherwise. Some stress that having the same neurology is all that is required for Miss Doll to be one of us: in some way, experiences are identical with brain events. A difficulty here is to grasp how our experiences pains, visual impressions and how things seem to us – can be just chemical or electrical changes in the brain. And why insist that creatures which lack our neural structures – maybe creatures from distant planets – cannot have experiences?

The way we assess whether others are in pain, keen for a drink or just happy, is not by their neurology but by what they do or say and tend to do and say. This leads some to identify experiences with behavioural tendencies. We may think that this approach muddles the way in which we *tell* whether something is so – for example, that someone is in pain – with its *being* so. If, though, this is the right approach, then, again, Miss Doll is definitely one of us. A difficulty here lies in making sense of the idea that my experience of pain simply is identical to a tendency to want to cry out and escape from the perceived cause. And, of course, 'wanting to cry' and 'perceiving' also need to be understood in ways related to further behavioural tendencies.

*　　　*　　　*

Miss Doll raises the questions of what minds and experiences are and how they relate to the body. How things seem and feel to me – do they not possess a privacy? My experiences cannot simply be physical events open to public gaze.

'What is it like to be a bat?' That question is one way of raising the difficulty. However much we humans learn about the behaviour and neural structures of bats, however much crazed philosophers hang upside down from church towers, flapping their arms, is there not something that we miss – namely, how *bats* experience the world? Plausibly, we should answer 'yes'; yet such an answer pushes us further, into thinking that we also can neither directly know how other humans experience the world nor, indeed, how we experienced it previously (nor, for that matter, whether other humans experience the world at all). Perhaps other humans are, in fact, nothing but many Miss Dolls, if Miss Doll is, indeed, nothing but a senseless robot.

Thus, we hit the problem of 'other minds'. If I possess direct knowledge of only one example of a mind, an experiencer, me, what can justify me in my firm belief that there are other experiencers? Can I even make sense of there being experiences other than mine? I know only *my* experiences. Can I make any sense at all of a mine/thine distinction? What do you think, Miss Doll?

'These ways madness lies. I thought (if I may use the term) that things were bad enough when you scientists and philosophers tried to persuade me that I lack all experiences. With this "other minds" problem, I may argue that I alone am the one individual who has experiences. Madness indeed. Let's try sense. I use words such as "experiences", "thinking" and "feelings" in the usual way. In view of that, it is impossible for me to grasp that my use is somehow phoney – and that, in fact, I lack experiences. I guess you have all been raising an empty problem for me.'

Miss Doll, if you are a senseless robot, then you are just parroting such words without any understanding of those words and with no experiences at all.

'And how do you know you're not?'

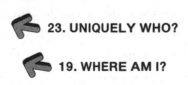

23. UNIQUELY WHO?

19. WHERE AM I?

30

EYE SPY

Abraham Bredius was a twentieth-century Dutch art historian, highly influential in his day. He specialized in paintings by the seventeenth-century artist, Jan Vermeer. In the late 1930s, a painting, *Christ and the Disciples at Emmaus*, came to light. Mindful of forgeries, Bredius and others closely examined the work, before hailing it as a genuine – and magnificent – Vermeer. They described the painting in glowing aesthetic terms, considering it Vermeer's finest achievement. The Boyman's Museum in Rotterdam bought the painting through a certain Han van Meegeren. Van Meegeren was delighted, not so much because of the money, but because he had successfully duped the experts. *The Disciples* was a van Meegeren, painted in the 1930s, not a Vermeer, painted in the 1600s. Such was the painting's quality that some experts of the day refused to believe van Meegeren, taking him to be faking it as a fake.

However, *The Disciples* is now firmly established as a van Meegeren; it is no Vermeer.

Sir A was another, more recent, influential art historian. He too was mindful of fakes. He was a friend of Eric Hebborn, a fine forger. It is unclear to what extent Sir A was taken in by Hebborn's fakes but in 1979 it came out that he – Sir Anthony Blunt, a long-serving and distinguished Director of the Courtauld Institute and Surveyor of the Queen's Pictures – had for many years been a Soviet spy.

When *The Disciples* was spied as fake, not merely the monetary value of the painting radically fell but so – for many – did its aesthetic value. No longer was it such a good painting. No longer was it displayed in the Boyman's.

When Sir Anthony was spied as fake 'loyal servant' of Britain, his integrity radically diminished; yet no one seriously thought his spying undermined his aesthetic credentials. The man was seen in a different light; his artistic perception was not. We may wonder whether his aesthetic judgements were as deceptive as his apparent loyalty to Britain but that would encourage assessment of those judgements on their merits. Their truth or falsity would not rest on their having been made by a Soviet spy.

A fake Vermeer can no longer be prized as by Vermeer. Once alerted to a painting's fake status, we may study it more closely, looking for aesthetic signs of the fakery, but why should merely being a fake detract from its aesthetic value? Aesthetic value rests on a work's colouring, composition, grace and beauty: how could it also rest, even partly, on its source?

Why is how you feel about a painting's quality affected by its being a fake?

Art experts, art lovers and, for that matter, the public in general, tend to feel that a fake is not as artistically valuable as 'the genuine thing'. Why?

There could be relevant aesthetic differences between originals and fakes, differences residing there, 'in the painting'. Now that the differences have been pointed out, we can see them – and we see them as detracting from the painting's quality. We may become aware that the composition is not so orderly or the figures not so gracefully drawn. However, in many cases of fakery, the defects are imperceptible, except under microscopes or through chemical analyses, so it is difficult to grasp what direct relevance they could have to our aesthetic appreciation. In the famous van Meegeren case, the painting's aesthetic qualities had been highly praised. It is true that experts today identify some compositional defects but those certainly were not seen at the time of van Meegeren's revelation and the painting's fall from grace.

A forgery often is an inferior work, compared to the master's originals. It may therefore be claimed – though without any good reason – that, somewhere along the line, some perceptible inferiority will, as a matter of fact, be spotted in any forgery. Let us, then, purify our example. Consider a case in which there is nothing in a painting that viewers can see which shows the work to be a fake or poor imitation. Consider a case in which the only differences between genuine Vermeers and the fake are factors to do with its underlying chemical composition, date of being painted and so on; experts with no knowledge of the discovery of the forgery would see the painting as a fine Vermeer. Aesthetically, nothing has changed with regard to the painting, once considered an original Vermeer but now known as a fake Vermeer – or so it would seem.

Moral evaluations are available. People have been deceived by the forger; the painting is key witness to the deception. Maybe some illegal transactions of 'passing off' have taken place. Yet why should such things matter aesthetically? Deception and illegality could be absent. A genuine misattribution of a painting to Vermeer could occur. The mistake is discovered – and the same puzzling consequences for the painting's painterly value flow forth. We need to look beyond the brush strokes for any plausible explanation of the relevance of fakery or misattribution to aesthetic valuations, yet such looking beyond seems immediately to take us away from the aesthetic valuations.

Returning to van Mcegeren's pretend Vermeer, the painting lacks many features of authentic Vermeers. It was neither handled by Vermeer, nor seen by his friends nor left in an unfinished state while he gazed upon it, wondering how to continue. We are not seeing a painting that Vermeer saw. It lacks those historical associations, those links to the past – and such associations and links often possess value for us. Witness the importance of wearing not a replica but the very watch given to you by your mother; of holding the original score by Bartok rather than a copy, or of standing in the actual room in King's College, Cambridge where Wittgenstein allegedly brandished the poker (noted in Chapter 28). But why should such associations and links concerning paintings possess *aesthetic* value?

Perhaps, when we look at a painting, valuing its composition, colour, texture and so on, we are also valuing it as manifesting an artist's creativity. Perhaps the artist's creativity can be seen in a painting. Forgeries are often straightforward copies, displaying the forger's skill but lacking originality. If so, how we see the painting changes. Compare how a line drawing may be seen solely as a duck, until someone points out that it is also a rabbit.

This approach, relying on creativity, fails to solve the problem of van Meegeren's 'Vermeer'. Van Meegeren's was an original composition, though painted in Vermeer's style. That it was painted in Vermeer's style should not itself undermine its originality and aesthetic value; for Vermeer's later paintings themselves manifested work in his style, yet are no less valuable because of that. Perhaps, paradoxically, van Meegeren's *The Disciples* should be seen as much as a Vermeer as Vermeer's own late Vermeers. Van Meegeren, when painting that painting, was showing what could be done with that style of painting as much as Vermeer did. Seeing it as a Vermeer should be no different aesthetically from seeing a Vermeer.

*   *   *

Sexton Blakes (rhyming slang for 'fakes') have often been successfully produced by the likes of van Meegeren, Hebborn and

Tom Keating. Hebborn claimed that some of his fakes still hang in galleries, undetected. Were their fakery discovered, they would be removed as mere copies. Yet, paradoxically, galleries sometimes cloak copies with the status of original art. An historically famous case is the 1917 Paris exhibition, which contained Duchamp's *Fountain*. This 'work of art' – the original – is just one white urinal among millions, save signed by Duchamp and displayed as an exhibit. This raises the puzzle of why one thing is a work of art when something indistinguishable from it, save for location, is not. Placed in the right setting, items such as Duchamp's urinal are works of art – or they are often taken to be such. Even though Duchamp's original was not made by him, that original exhibit is the valuable *Fountain* and a completely indistinguishable copy will not do.

Perhaps what carries the greatest artistic value is the art gallery, for its embrace can turn almost anything into art. Maybe the next exhibit for the British Turner Prize should itself be an art gallery such as Tate Britain, Tate Modern or a Guggenheim. If only it were easy to pop a Tate into a Tate, even a full-blown copy of a Tate into a Tate – and if only I were under forty – I would exhibit it myself for the prize . . . or exhibit even myself.

 8. WILL YOU STILL LOVE ME TOMORROW?

2. FICTIONAL FEELINGS?

31

DON'T READ THIS NOTICE

Unthinking students often ask in lectures, 'May I ask a question?' Quick and witted replies are 'Too late' and 'Was that the question?'

If the 'Don't read this notice' sign refers to itself, then it too is too late in its warning, just as is the notice that says 'Do not enter the blue room,' which is displayed in the blue room rather than outside. Do such thoughts help us to handle a couple of paradoxical classics?

There once was a barber, of Alcala, a Sicilian village, who, it was famously said, shaved all those inhabitants of the village who did not shave themselves. It was added that he shaved no others; he shaved only those who did not shave themselves – and he shaved all of them. So far, so good, until someone asked, 'Did the barber shave himself?'

Either he did or he did not. Suppose he shaved himself: then he was not one of the inhabitants who did not shave themselves. But we are told that the barber shaved *only* those who did not shave themselves. So, he did not shave himself. Therefore, from the supposition that he did shave himself it follows that he did not — which is a contradiction. 'Con-tra-diction!' we could sing. Presumably, then, he did not shave himself; so let us consider this alternative. If he did not shave himself, then he was one of those inhabitants who did not shave themselves, but as we are told that the barber did shave all such inhabitants, he must therefore have shaved himself. 'Con-tra-diction!'

What is to be done? It is not possible for there to be a barber who both does and does not shave himself. When we said that either the barber shaved himself or did not, we were presupposing that such a barber existed. The answer is that there can be no such barber. The presupposition is false.

And now for something completely different — or is it? It derives from Eubulides but a closely similar problem is associated with the centuries earlier Epimenides. Both were of Ancient Greece.

Suppose someone says, 'I'm lying' — and says nothing else. When people utter such words, they are typically referring to other things that they have said; but in this case the speaker is referring solely to what he is saying when saying, 'I'm lying.'

Is the speaker who just says 'I'm lying' speaking the truth?

As with the Barber, let us consider the two alternatives: that he is speaking the truth and that he is not. Suppose he is speaking the truth: then it is true that he is lying but if he is lying, he is not speaking the truth. We have a contradiction. Suppose that he is not speaking the truth: then, as we assume he knows what he is doing, he is lying and so, as he says that he is lying, he is speaking the truth after all. 'Con-tra-diction!'

With the Barber, we said that there could be no barber. With the Liar?

The speaker who says that he is lying both exists and utters the words 'I'm lying' but we may reasonably challenge the assumption that he expresses something that is true or false. Just as the Barber paradox led us to conclude that there could be no such barber, so the Liar paradox may lead us to conclude that there is nothing that is being expressed by the speaker which is either true or false.

This answer does not reach the heart of the problem, for we can strengthen the paradox, with the speaker saying that what he says is not true. Would he not be expressing the truth that what he says is not true? If so, again the contradiction arises. This has suggested to some that we should resort to a stronger claim, namely that there is nothing at all that such a speaker is expressing when he says, 'What I am saying right now is not true' – despite the words forming a coherent sentence. We need to handle this response with care. Quite what grip have we on the notion of 'expressing' such that we can tell that such a speaker is expressing nothing at all? He certainly seems to be expressing something more than someone who is silent or who utters nonsense words. Let us leave that thought lingering, to be picked up later.

*　　*　　*

A notice can sensibly instruct people not to read a different notice, just as the sign that warns of dangers in the blue room can be sensibly placed outside the blue room. Futility arises when the notices involve elements of self-reference. A barber in Alcala can readily shave all and only those who do not shave themselves in the next village, say, Balcala. The contradiction arises if that barber moves to Balcala. Metaphorically, he goes up in a puff of smoke or a froth of shaving soap. In more literal mode, were the barber to move from Alcala to Balcala, then what was true of him about his shaving clientele could no longer be true.

A liar may say of someone else, without paradox, that that someone else is lying; it is when he says it of himself that paradox flies forth. True, he may sincerely think that he expresses something but he is merely uttering words and failing to express a complete thought. By analogy, someone is not successfully telling you the meaning of 'blibble' if, when asked what she means, she can say only that by 'blibble' she means 'blibble'.

Notices and sayings usually need to point away from themselves, rather than referring to themselves, but we need to be wary of mirrorings; wary of what is said being reflected back, indirectly generating some self-reference.

(1) What I express by the next sentence is true.
(2) What I expressed by the previous sentence is not true.

The first sentence is used to tell us about what is expressed by the second but that sends us scuttling back to the first, with paradoxical results – unless we insist, once again, that, one way or another, nothing is being expressed.

Self-reference continues to feast philosophers' minds. Some self-reference seems fine. For example, this sentence is printed in black. My use of that sentence expressed a truth. But we may question whether that sentence involves self-reference. What is expressed is about the sentence (the printing) used; it is not about what is expressed by means of that sentence; that is, it is not about itself. What is expressed is not the sort of thing that can be coloured. A word can be printed in black but the meaning of a word cannot be printed at all. The same belief may be expressed by both German and French speakers, but their utterances would be radically different – as is sometimes the case with the English and American, to say nothing of the differing sounds from a Glaswegian and Geordie who are yet expressing identical views.

When a speaker announces, 'What I am saying right now is not true,' quite what is it that he is saying is not true? It is whatever is referred to by his use of 'What I am saying right now'. But what is that? It is not the words but whatever is expressed by the words. But what is expressed? It seems that we are in a position akin to the emptiness of 'blibble'; there is nothing there that is being spoken about. We may now clarify the claim that nothing is expressed by the use of such self-referential sentences. The truth is that nothing is identified which the speaker is expressing anything about. Although some things are being expressed – for example the concepts of 'saying' and 'being true' are being expressed – they are not being expressed *about* anything. There is nothing there to express anything about.

What has just been said may be interesting – or uninteresting. But is what is expressed by means of this sentence interesting?

 4. HE WOULD SAY THAT, WOULDN'T HE?

 14. DON'T TELL HIM, PIKE!

 12. IT'S ALL RELATIVE . . . ISN'T IT?

32

MYSTERIES

'Once upon a time, there was nothing . . .'

It is not a tale easy to develop. If we continue with '. . . and then there was something', many would ask, 'How did that something pop into existence? Popped into existence from nothing, did it?' All that we could sensibly reply is, 'It just did.' But that feels inadequate. Some physicists have spoken of the laws of nature 'holding', yet then we should wonder what sense can be made of such laws holding, when there is nothing; we should wonder what is the explanation of there being such laws, rather than none.

Let us try our tale again.

'Once upon a time, there was something . . .'

Now we have something to get our teeth into but many will wonder, 'So how did that something come about?' To that question we may give some answers that momentarily satisfy. We may announce that the something was brought about by something else – and that something else by something else further and so on . . . That passes the explanatory buck. Whether or not such 'bringing it about' chains can go on, back and back, without a beginning, there yet remains the question of how such chains, endless or not, came to exist, rather than nothing at all.

Let us try starting our tale for a third time.

'Once upon a time, there was everything . . .'

Now, we probably tend to worry about the 'Once upon a time' over which, so far, we have been silent. We may well point out that not everything is present just at the one time; there are all the things that went before that time and all the things that come after that time – all the things past and all those future. We may muse upon whether only the present exists or whether the past and present exist but not the future – or whether past, present and future all exist. Let us avoid such complexities here.

'Once upon a time' tales possess movement, usually telling us how some events came about as a result of others. So, we could revise our beginning yet again.

'Once upon a time, there was everything that had been up to and including, that time . . .'

Why are there all the things that there are?

Why were there all the things that there were?

These questions can be raised even if the 'all the things' includes a 'never-ending' chain of somethings having been brought about. The questions could be expanded by adding 'and why all the things that there will be?'

The questions could be divided into 'Why is there – why was there – anything at all?' and 'Why are the things that there are (and were) just those things with those properties?' Let us stay with the first question. In one understanding, it is a question that is frequently asked, in the highest and lowest of circles, with answers demanded and sometimes given. In another understanding, it is one that is shuffled around, in the highest and lowest of circles, with no answer really demanded and no good, clear answer given. The two understandings hang on the 'all' or 'everything'.

The first understanding is that 'everything' covers the whole universe, that is, everything that scientists study: stars, planets, electricity, playstations, cars, central heating, men, women and treacle tart – all things, including minds, including institutions such as money, the law and morality. A terminological complexity needs to be noted: in recent years, a few philosophers, followed by some physicists, have suggested that maybe many universes exist. Our use of 'universe' covers the whole lot.

When 'everything' is so understood, the question is asked, 'How or why did "everything" come about?' Even if the 'everything' consists of a series of things that has no beginning, why is there a series at all? Many feel that to be a genuine question and that, without an answer, we are collapsed into mystery. Many are led to say that, therefore, there must be a creator God (or gods). They say that only with the existence of a creator can the universe's existence be intelligible.

The second understanding is this. 'Everything' is taken, curiously (!), to mean everything. It covers the universe but also any gods or God that exists. How did 'everything', understood really to include everything, come about? Strangely, that does not trouble some people. Their answer is that a creator God (or, maybe, gods), part of the everything, just *had* to exist – and created the rest. Maybe the universe just happens to be, but not God. God *must* be. I and you might not have existed; we are contingent beings, not necessary beings. Had our parents not engaged in funny bodily dealings one day (or, more likely, night) we should not have existed. With God it is different. His existence is not contingent on anything outside of him. He exists necessarily.

How can there, though, be something that *has* to be? Sometimes the answer is that it is a mystery. 'So much,' we may be tempted to reply, 'for telling us that we need to accept God to make intelligible the seeming mystery of the universe's existence.' If we suggest that perhaps the universe itself had to be, with no need of God, heads are shaken: that would indeed be a mystery. But would it? Is it any more mysterious than the mystery of a necessarily existing creator God who moves in mysterious ways?

Maybe these puzzling thoughts arise because of our expectations from explanations. Leibniz adopted the principle of sufficient reason: there must be a sufficient reason for everything. When we give reasons – or explanations – we go beyond what it is that we are giving reasons for. We explain A by reference to B and B by reference to C and so on. So, when we are successful in giving an explanation, inevitably there pops up reference to something else and hence a need for another explanation, one of that something else. The resort to a creator God is recognition that explanations must come to an end; but once that is recognized, there should be no need to look for a creator of the universe at all. Maybe the universe just happens to be.

*   *   *

If this universe just happens to be, might there indeed have been nothing? Or must there always have been some universe but not necessarily this particular one?

That there might have been nothing is a dizzy thought. When we try to imagine nothing, we probably remove, in our thinking, all the items from the universe, yet are we not still left with space and time? How can we remove those? Yet just because we cannot imagine 'nothing' – if it is true that we cannot – it does not follow that there might not have been nothing.

Might there have been empty space and time? Let us focus on time. What counts as time passing, if there are no changes going on at all; no clocks ticking; no movements of electrons; no hearts beating? Perhaps time requires the existence of events, of happenings. And, surely, events and happenings need to take place in time.

Could there have been something that is neither in space nor time? Some tell us that God is neither spatial nor temporal. Maybe we do have a grip on such spacelessness and timelessness: numbers, if they exist at all, do not exist in space or at a particular time. However, if God is timeless, then there is another mystery, namely how God could be a creator, for creating is an event, a happening, which takes place in time. Numbers do not create things; God is usually taken to have created things.

There are further mysteries. One that comes to the fore is whether time itself has a beginning. It certainly could not have had a beginning in time but if time stretches back without end, infinitely, does that mean that an infinite series of time durations, that is, an endless series, must have been completed by now? How is that possible?

Even if something could exist that needs no explanation, some have insisted that an explanation is required of how there is this *particular* something – the universe with conscious and (occasionally) intelligent life. Is it not highly unlikely that this should have come about without intelligent design?

I am not sure that we have any grip on what is likely or unlikely when we are talking of the universe, of which we know so little and of which there is only one. Whatever we conclude about that likelihood, why is the universe's just happening to exist so less likely than a creator God creating this universe? No doubt we shall continue to be told that God moves in mysterious ways but then it is a mystery why the God mystery is considered less mysterious than the universe's existence mystery.

Enough of these dancing mysteries for this chapter. Mystery mongering must come to an end, as must explanations – though that does remind me . . .

How do we end our tales? 'In the end, things just stop.' 'In the end, there will be nothing.' 'In the end there is no end.' The focus is usually on the beginning of 'everything' but maybe there are similar puzzles to do with the end of 'everything'. More mystery mongering indeed.

It is time to end – but, paradoxically, we have one more chapter to go.

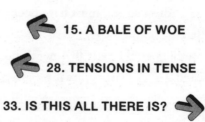

◄ 15. A BALE OF WOE

◄ 28. TENSIONS IN TENSE

33. IS THIS ALL THERE IS? ►

33

IS THIS ALL THERE IS?

You awake one morning, alone. Your family and friends are lost, forgotten or are no more. No longer do they matter: no longer does anything matter, save one thing: the itch. The itch nags away, just below your shoulder-blades, right in the middle of your back. It distracts you from all else. It irritates; it puts you on edge. Devilish torturers would create such itchy sensations, just to see you wriggle, while they prevented you from scratching. You twist your arm, stretching and straining – and just about, yes, just about, you manage to scratch. What a delicious sensation, that scratch. And what relief from the itch. What amazing relief!

Consider two continuations of this tale, *Discontented* and *Contented*.

Discontented: What amazing relief! – yet 'tis short-lived. Another itch starts up. Once again, you twist and turn, scratch and dig at your skin. Once again, peace returns but only momentarily, for, yet again, an itch starts up. And, as soon as that itch is quelled, yet more arise, criss-crossing, of differing degree, tingle and tickle, of different shadings of irritation and location. As they arise, you writhe and wriggle, squirm and scratch. And so life goes on . . . and on . . . and on . . . Itch and scratch, itch and scratch, itch . . .

Contented: What amazing relief! Contentment warms your body, the distressful itch having vanished. You bask in the feeling of bliss. Yet it quickly subsides, leaving you satisfied by absence of itch; but that is all. Nothing else stirs within you: no hopes, no desires and no curiosity. And the sun rises, crosses the sky and sets. Nothing is left to thwart you . . .

What more is there to life than either the *Discontented* or the *Contented*?

Life is a kaleidoscope of pains and pleasures, despairs and hopes, family and friends, careers and games, loves and luck, learning and failures, and health and illness; not mere itches and scratches. But do not all these things come down to itching and scratching? Are not itching and scratching representative of what goes on in life? All the things mentioned in our list are, ultimately, matters involving having some discontent (itches) to overcome and (if we are lucky?) the overcoming (scratching) which provides relief. What is the value in that?

If contentment only arises through overcoming discontent, would not states without the initial discontent be preferable? Yet such states seem to be totally without point – as pointless as being a pebble is to a pebble. Human that we are, however, even contentments usually (and pretty quickly) become transformed into discontentments of boredom. Maybe, after all, a pebble is better off, having none of these states.

Why is human existence preferable to a pebble's?

In the nineteenth century, Schopenhauer, known as the 'philosopher of pessimism', stressed the suffering of human life: either we want something that we lack or we have got what we wanted. Either way, we suffer – through the lack of what we want or through boredom from the lack of want, now having what we wanted. True, a multitude of different wants may criss-cross; we may be satisfied (or not) at different times, but a mishmash of sufferings and boredoms does not detract from the suffering and boredom. If Schopenhauer is right, would it not be better to be a pebble, lacking all experiences? Were we just pebbles on a beach, all life's waves and turmoils would (dare I quip?) wash over us.

Schopenhauer is wrong, at least in the specifics. With many things, we simply enjoy the activity of overcoming the dissatisfactions. As is often said, 'tis better to travel hopefully than to arrive.

It is a mistake to think that if we deploy means to an end, the means are irrelevant, lacking all value in themselves, and it is the end alone that matters. Our goal may be to reach the top of Mount Everest but we do not want to reach it by just any means. We want to climb the mountain, do battle with blizzards, struggle on, up and up. When (in my case, better to say 'if') we reach the top, we have achieved our goal and by the right means. Achievements are measured not solely by the outcomes but by how they were achieved. To find ourselves transported to Everest's summit by helicopter or at the press of a button would lose the appeal of achievement, unless the sought achievement was that of managing successfully to fly the helicopter or to build a machine that could whisk people from A to B at a button's press.

Schopenhauer may be right in his pessimism, in as far as most lives involve more sufferings than satisfactions. Many sufferings seem more or less inevitable – even for those who are life's winners. There are losses of family, friends and lovers; awareness of the increasing disabilities likely in old age; and, in all likelihood, direct experience of those disabilities ourselves one day and for some years – and then the pains of dying. There is awareness of the sufferings of millions of others, past, present and future and the sufferings of animals. Further, some of us grow deeply attached even to objects – a book, a gown, a much loved car – sometimes even ascribing them a life of their own, with resultant distress when they too collapse, worn with old age. With such reflections, we may well agree that the happiest are, so to speak, those never to have been born.

* * *

What is the point of it all? Many cannot resist asking that question. There are points and purposes in my life – but what is the point or purpose of my life?

Some answer by explaining how their lives gain point through helping their children, working to improve lives of the poor or advancing some political cause. But this is passing the purpose buck: what is the point of the children's lives or the political cause? Whatever answer is given, we may ask a similar question. Some turn to the hope of an eternal afterlife but that too has no more ultimate point than a finite life. If there is a genuine question to be asked about the point of a finite life, there is also a question about the point of an infinitely long life. Before we pop in the answer 'serving God' or similar, we should be aware that we may then ask: what is the point of such service and of God's existence?

Perhaps we should come to realize that, for something to have value, there need not be a point to it. That is one way of answering Chapter 2's final question on the point of certain plays, music and literature. Mind you, the point of saying that valuable things need have no point may be to pre-empt those about to ask the point of philosophy. To that question, though, some answers can be given. For one thing, philosophy enables us to appreciate that various activities may possess value even though without point. Philosophy also shows itself to be an activity, an intrinsically valuable activity; that is, many of us value it for its own sake.

Lives may be valuable, not least because they are lives of valuers who value features of the universe, life and living. True, lives end; but could we even face eternal living? Awareness of dying enfolds many with bleak and haunting melancholies of

'What's the point?' Let us remember that there can be no point beyond all points. Points must come to an end just as must explanations.

All the things we value, however rare, however small, that give point or meaning to our lives – the friendships, loves and absurdities; those soundscaped memories entwined with shared passions and glances that magically ensnare and enfold; the intoxications of wines and words, and wayward musings and music, with which we wrestle into misty slumbering nights, our senses revived by sparkling waters, much needed at dawn; the seascapes of wild waves, mysterious moonlights and images and widening skies that stretch the eyes – do indeed all cease to exist; and curiously the most enchanting are oft those within which we lose ourselves and also cease to be – yet that they, and we, existed at some time remains timelessly true, outside of all time.

For lovers of eternity, that is as good as it gets.

Blow, bugle, blow,
set the wild echoes flying;
And answer, echoes,
answer, dying,
dying, dying.

(Tennyson)

APPENDIX

Further reading

Fine introductions to philosophy generally and to ethics in particular are, respectively, Simon Blackburn's *Think* (Oxford: OUP, 1999) and *Being Good* (Oxford: OUP, 2001). A distinctive but more difficult introductory text is Bernard Williams' *Morality: An Introduction to Ethics* (Cambridge: CUP, 1972). An excellent survey of applied ethics' problems is Jonathan Glover's *Causing Death and Saving Lives* (London: Penguin, 1977) and, of God, Nick Everitt's *The Non-Existence of God* (London: Routledge, 2004). For some favouring of God, see T. J. Mawson's *Belief in God* (Oxford: OUP, 2005). When politics enters the fray, see Jonathan Wolff's *An Introduction to Political Philosophy* (Oxford: OUP, 1996). A brief survey of some religious, ethical and political matters is my *Humanism: A Beginner's Guide* (Oxford: Oneworld, forthcoming).

The best clear reference work to philosophical problems typically labelled 'paradoxes' – so it excludes many problems discussed here but includes many, more formal paradoxes – is Michael Clark's *Paradoxes from A to Z*, 2nd ed. (London: Routledge, 2007). Another good survey of numerous paradoxes, including some trivial, is Nicholas Rescher's *Paradoxes: Their Roots, Range and Resolution* (Chicago: Open Court, 2001). For an historical, entertaining and idiosyncratic approach, try Roy Sorensen's *A Brief History of the Paradox* (New York: OUP, 2003). A detailed study of some core paradoxes is R. M. Sainsbury's *Paradoxes*, 2nd ed. (Cambridge: CUP, 1995). An accessible and appealing introduction to logic, applying it to some themes here, is Graham Priest's *Logic: A Very Short Introduction* (Oxford: OUP, 2000). An attempt at an entertaining radio series, deploying some of the puzzles, was made by me for BBC Radio 4, broadcast in 2005 as *This Sentence Is False*. Who knows if it could ever be revived or revised?

Additional readings, varying in difficulty and accessibility, are given in 'Notes, sources and references'. The first place to start, for introductory material, is the relevant work above. Readers who worry about terms such as 'contradiction', 'essential', 'metaphysics', would wisely consult Thomas Mautner's *Dictionary of Philosophy*, 2nd ed. (London: Penguin Books, 2005) or the more comprehensive work, ed. Robert Audi, *The Cambridge Dictionary of Philosophy* (Cambridge: CUP, 1995). The latter also provides useful introductions to the major philosophers mentioned in the puzzles.

Popular philosophy magazines and journals are *Philosophy Now,* *The Philosophers Magazine* and *Think.* Their websites are easily spotted by googling. Some information is also sometimes available at www.petercave.com. An excellent online philosophy encyclopaedia is Stanford University's www.seop.leeds.ac.uk/contents.html. There are many philosophy meetings open to the public and not solely in London. See, for example, www.sas.ac.uk and www.royalinstitutephilosophy.org. Do not be afraid of going along.

Notes, sources and references

Preface

The Monty Hall Show's solution is: you, the contestant, should always switch, for you thereby improve your chances of winning from one-third to two-thirds. Think through the single case. You initially chose A, with one-third winning chance. If you stay with A, you stay with the one third chance; you know that at least one of the other doors hides a goat. Had you been able to select *both* B and C, you would, of course, have secured a two-thirds chance of winning. Had you to choose randomly between B and C, you would remain just at the one-third chance. The commère, though, has shown that door B should not be chosen; hence, in choosing C, you increase your winning chance to two-thirds. Try this: if you play the game many times, you would expect to lose in two-thirds of them but by always switching, all those losing games become winning games; this is because the commère's revelation ensures that, in those games, you always avoid goats, the commère always having to open the remaining goat door, thus guiding you to the correct door. It is true that, with regard to those cases when your original choices would have made you a winner, in changing your choices you then lose – but those cases occur in just one-third of the games.

For sceptical readers, let me point out that a computer simulation has apparently been run of the game many thousands of times, with the result that changing the selection increased the winning as stated. Further discussion is in Clark (see 'Further reading').

John Maynard Keynes (1883–1946) is the well-known Cambridge economist. It is little-known that earlier he worked on philosophy, writing *A Treatise on Probability* (London: Macmillan, 1921), from whence the quotation in the text derives, p. 427.

Wittgenstein (1889–1951) was the tormented genius, encouraged by Keynes and others – not to be tormented but to return to Cambridge and philosophize anew. See Ray Monk's fascinating biography, *Ludwig Wittgenstein: The Duty of Genius* (London: Jonathan Cape, 1990). 'I'll teach you differences' is from Shakespeare's *King Lear*.

Aristotle (384–322 BCE) vies with Plato (428–347 BCE) for being considered the greatest ancient Greek philosopher. Aristotle studied under Plato; Plato sat at the feet of Socrates, presumably when Socrates was not in motion. See Bernard

Williams' slender introduction, *Plato: The Invention of Philosophy* (London: Phoenix, 1998), for an insight into early philosophical perplexities.

Chapter 1 The dangers of health

This raises a classic problem for utilitarianism; similar problems haunt other moral theories. There is a vast literature. See J. J. C. Smart and Bernard Williams, *Utilitarianism: For and Against* (Cambridge, CUP, 1973). Peter Singer's work, *Practical Ethics*, 2nd ed. (Cambridge: CUP, 1993), provides an accessible and wide-ranging utilitarian approach. A very small introductory collection on John Stuart Mill, edited by me, is *John Stuart Mill on . . .* (London: British Humanist Association, 2006). The great utilitarian who influenced Mill is Jeremy Bentham: see his waxed skeleton, sitting in a cabinet, at University College London. There are more references to Mill's works in Chapters 3, 13 and 26.

Chapter 2 Fictional feelings?

Recent discussion of these paradoxes was initiated by Colin Radford's 'How Can We Be Moved by the Fate of Anna Karenina?' reprinted in Alex Neill and Aaron Ridley's *Arguing About Art*, 2nd ed. (London: Routledge, 2002). The collection also contains paradoxes of horror, tragedy and suspense. Aristotle discusses tragedy in his *Poetics* (many editions). The complexity of fiction and reality being intertwined with opera's incongruities is manifested in, for example, John Adams' opera *Nixon in China*. Look out for the production by Peter Sellars.

Chapter 3 Sympathy for the Devil

This is a satire, in accord with a Rolling Stones' title, of the traditional problem of evil. For detailed discussions, see Marilyn McCord Adams and Robert Merrihew Adams, eds., *The Problem of Evil* (Oxford: OUP, 1990). John Stuart Mill's discussion of God's nature is in his 'Nature', in *Three Essays on Religion* (Buffalo: Prometheus Books, 1998).

Chapter 4 He would say that, wouldn't he?

The Machiavelli puzzles occur in my 'Humour and Paradox Laid Bare', in the journal *The Monist*, 88.1 (Peru, Illinois: The Hegeler Inst., 2005). Machiavelli offers his advice in *The Prince* (many editions). See notes to Chapter 1 for utilitarianism.

Mandy Rice-Davies' comment, more accurately, was 'He would, wouldn't he?' – a lighter moment in the 1960s British scandal concerning John Profumo's sexual dalliances. Profumo was Secretary of State for Defence in Macmillan's government. The establishment closed ranks, treating a certain Stephen Ward so appallingly that he committed suicide. Where does the moral responsibility lie in such cases?

Chapter 5 Therapy for tortoises

'Achilles and the tortoise' is one of Zeno's arguments against motion. Zeno (of Elea), *c.* 470 BCE, was a follower of Parmenides. For information on the Eleatic philosophers, see J. Barnes, *The Presocratic Philosophers*, vol. I (London: Routledge,

1979). For my take on the tortoise, see my 'With and Without End' in the journal, *Philosophical Investigations*, 30.2 (Oxford: Blackwell, 2007).

Chapter 6 *In the beginning*

Discussions of the ethics of abortion are in Glover (see 'Further reading'). For wide-ranging work on selves, see Derek Parfit's highly original *Reasons and Persons* (Oxford: OUP, 1984). Delightful little satires – note 'Ivan Kudovbin' – are in Michael Frayn's collection of his 1960s columns, *The Original Michael Frayn* (London: Methuen, 1983). Frayn read philosophy, then known as 'moral sciences', in 1950s Cambridge. A light dialogue involving Herm is my 'Herm and Matt', *Philosophy Now*, 41 (London: May 2003).

Chapter 7 *The innocent murderer: a nobody dunit*

The case of Phillips and Daniels occurred some decades ago; I can remember neither details nor names, but it is the philosophical gist that matters. Some legal oddities are in Peter Seddon's *The Law's Strangest Cases* (London: Robson Books, 2001). Problems of action identification were brought to the fore by the splendid and idiosyncratic Elisabeth Anscombe, distinguished pupil of Wittgenstein. See G. E. M. Anscombe, *Intention* (Oxford: Blackwell, 1957). Catharine A. MacKinnon's *Only Words* (London: HarperCollins, 1994) suggests that the portrayal of rape is rape.

Chapter 8 Will you still love me tomorrow?

Plato provided the picture of fortunate lovers being those who find their other half. Read Aristophanes' speech in Plato's *Symposium* (many editions). My erotic fictionalism still needs to be fleshed out but see my 'Sex Without God', in the journal *Think* 12 (London: TPM, Spring 2006), for a brief survey of sexual matters, from which this chapter derives. A full investigation is Roger Scruton's *Sexual Desire* (London: Weidenfeld & Nicolson, 1986). Scruton writes in a stimulating and provocative way. He supports fox-hunting.

Chapter 9 Sand, sun, sea and . . .

These are often known as 'sorites' or 'heap' puzzles ('sorites' being a Greek term meaning the same as 'heap'). Sorites puzzles are associated historically with Eubulides (mentioned in Chapter 31's notes). A good comprehensive collection (though not an easy read) is Rosanna Keefe and Peter Smith, eds., *Vagueness: A Reader* (Cambridge, Mass.: MIT Press, 1997).

Chapter 10 Mary, Mary, quite contrary

On these matters, see Gary Watson's *Free Will*, 2nd ed. (Oxford: OUP, 2003). G. E. M. Anscombe has discussed the relationship between 'cause', 'determine' and 'reason'; see her *Collected Philosophical Papers Volume II: Metaphysics and the Philosophy of Mind* (Oxford: Basil Blackwell, 1981). It is not easy going. My approach derives from Gilbert Ryle who was influenced by Wittgenstein. Ryle was philosophy's kingmaker in mid-twentieth-century Oxford, yet, somewhat to his chagrin, he became eclipsed by J. L. Austin (see notes to Chapter 14). Ryle's writing can be sparkling and entertaining. Try his *The Concept of Mind* (London: Penguin, 1990), where he coined the 'ghost in the machine', ridiculing Descartes' defence of the mind as an immaterial substance.

Jean-Paul Sartre (1905–1980) promoted the existentialist angst of free choices, of needing to take responsibility for our choices. The most accessible route into Sartre is his *Existentialism and Humanism*, trans. Philip Mairet (London: Methuen, 1948), though be warned that Sartre repudiated some parts.

Chapter 11 Just hanging around

The source of this paradox, often known as 'surprise hanging' or 'surprise examination', is a Second World War Scandinavian broadcast. It has generated much discussion. See Sorensen in notes to Chapter 14. For my take, see my 'Reeling and A-Reasoning: Surprise Examinations and Newcomb's Tale', in the Royal Institute of Philosophy's journal, *Philosophy*, 79.310 (Cambridge: CUP, 2004). For the cards' example, see Ardon Lyon's 'The Prediction Paradox', in the journal *Mind*, 68 NS (Oxford: Basil Blackwell, 1959).

Chapter 12 It's all relative . . . isn't it?

There are different readings of *Sharia* law. Lest some readers doubt the reality of such appalling treatment, see the Amnesty

International website reports. I use the *Sharia* law case because it is in the public eye. I am well aware that appalling treatments sometimes result from secular and Christian beliefs. On stoning, see the Amnesty report, MDE 13/095/2006, on the Iranian Penal Code. Article 102 states that men will be buried up to their waists and women their breasts, for stoning. Article 104 states, concerning adultery, that stones used should 'not be large enough to kill the person by one or two strikes nor should they be so small that they could not be defined as stones.'

Protagoras (*c.* 490–420 BCE) was the famous Greek sophist – a sophist, then, being an expert. Aristotle described Protagoras as someone who could make the weaker argument appear stronger – a good rhetorician. Barristers and politicians should applaud. Philosophers prefer to think of themselves as different – as seekers after truth, rather than argument winners. The classic discussion of relativism is Plato's *Theaetetus* (many editions). For a rejection of relativism, see Thomas Nagel's, *The Last Word* (Oxford: OUP, 1997). A detailed treatment, with references from cultural relativists and similar, is Maria Baghranian's *Relativism* (London: Routledge, 2004).

Chapter 13 Wolves, whistles and women

Writings on women as sex objects are often by feminist thinkers, such as Andrea Dworkin and Catharine MacKinnon. See Louise M. Antony and Charlotte W. Witt, eds., *A Mind of One's Own* (Boulder: Westview Press, 1993). The exuberance of some feminist writings may lead us into thinking that all intercourse is sometimes claimed to be akin to rape but the considered position presumably is not so sweeping.

Roger Scruton's *Sexual Desire* (see Chapter 8's notes) discusses sex objects. The great Immanuel Kant (1724–1804) tells of the lemon that has been sucked dry in his *Lectures on Ethics*, trans. L. Infield (New York: Harper and Row, 1963); marriage rights are discussed in his *Metaphysics of Morals*, trans. Mary Gregor (Cambridge: CUP, 1991). John Stuart Mill's Liberty Principle (also known as the 'Harm Principle') is put forward in his *On Liberty* (many editions). A discussion of Mill and sexual equality is in *John Stuart Mill on* . . .; see Chapter 1's notes.

Chapter 14 Don't tell him, Pike!

Moore's Paradox is much discussed. Variations on the theme and on the surprise hanging are within Roy Sorensen's *Blindspots* (Oxford: Clarendon, 1988). The link between Moore's Paradox and the surprise hanging is in Laurence Goldstein's 'Inescapable Surprises and Acquirable Intentions', in the journal *Analysis* 53 (Oxford: Basil Blackwell, 1993). See also his lively Wittgenstein introduction (with a somewhat distinctive style), namely, *Clear and Queer Thinking* (London, Duckworth, 1999). For more on Moore and other paradoxes, see my paper cited in Chapter 4's notes. Wittgenstein's original discussion is in his *Philosophical Investigations* (Oxford: Basil Blackwell, 1953), Part II §x. A detailed early investigation into performatives is J. L. Austin's *How To Do Things With*

Words, 2nd ed. (Oxford: Clarendon Press, 1975). Austin was the key figure in 1950s Oxford linguistic philosophy. Look out for his delightful quips.

Chapter 15 A bale of woe

The puzzle is traditionally attributed (probably wrongly) to Jean Buridan (*c*.1295–1360), who taught in Paris and was fond of asinine examples.

Spinoza (1632–1677) and Leibniz (1646–1716) were important seventeenth-century thinkers. Spinoza was associated with pantheism, influencing Romantics such as Coleridge, Shelley and Wordsworth. Leibniz was the eminent mathematician and philosopher, most popularly known for his quip about this being the best of all possible worlds. For humans being asinine, if unable to choose, see Spinoza's *Ethics* (Appendix to Part II). Leibniz's principle of sufficient reason is in, for example, 'On the Ultimate Origination of Things'. See the collection of Leibniz's writings edited by G. H. R. Parkinson (London: J M Dent, 1973).

Chapter 16 Just helping ourselves

Thomas Hobbes (1588–1679) is famous for his political work, *Leviathan*. The tale about Hobbes is from John Aubrey: see *Aubrey's Brief Lives* (various editions). Hobbes' exact position is open to scholarly debate. For promotion of genetic explanations of behaviour, see Richard Dawkins, *The Selfish Gene*, new ed. (Oxford: OUP, 2006). Dawkins' original presentation and his approach have been attacked by Mary Midgley. See her later *Evolution as a Religion* (London: Routledge, 2002).

Chapter 17   Girl, cage, chimp

Testing on chimps occurs in many countries, including the USA, but has been banned over the last decade in the European Union, though testing on other primates and other animals continues apace. 'Speciesism' was introduced by Richard Ryder but made famous by Peter Singer in, for example, his *Practical Ethics* (see Chapter 1's notes). Singer defends animal *liberation* rather than animal *rights*. Contrast with Tom Regan's *The Case for Animal Rights* (Berkeley: University of California Press, 1983). An accessible survey, covering Bentham, Singer, Regan and Midgley's 'family-ism' quip, is Rosalind Hursthouse's *Ethics, Humans and Other Animals* (London: Routledge, 2000). Hursthouse is a good place to start. A little known early thinker, who speaks of animal rights, is Henry Salt. See George Hendrick and Willene Hendrick, eds., *The Savour of Salt* (Fontwell: Centaur Press, 1989). Let me encourage Salt savouring.

Chapter 18   Vote! Vote! Vote?

Detailed discussion is by Jonathan Glover in 'It Makes No Difference Whether Or Not I Do It', reprinted in Peter Singer, ed., *Applied Ethics* (Oxford: OUP, 1986). A more general discussion of democracy is Ross Harrison's *Democracy* (London: Routledge, 1993).

Chapter 19 Where am I?

Descartes (1596–1650) presented his dreaming scepticism and the evil genius hypothesis in the first two meditations of his *Meditations on First Philosophy* (many editions). Descartes deploys scepticism, doubting as far as he can, but is not himself a sceptic. He uses scepticism to overcome scepticism and rebuild his knowledge. For an introductory approach, see Timothy Chappell's *The Inescapable Self* (London: Weidenfeld & Nicolson, 2005). An original work, praised as extraordinary and challenging, is J. J. Valberg's *Dream, Death, and the Self* (Princeton NJ: Princeton University Press, 2007). Although I have seen little more than the cover – the book has only just appeared – the sighting was through no glass darkly, but clear Pinot Grigio. I am confident that it (the book) merits considerable attention.

Chapter 20 Out of time

Many temporal problems were brought to the fore by Derek Parfit, referred to in Chapter 6. That we should be no more concerned about our future non-existence than about our pre-birth non-existence goes back to the Athenian Epicurus (*c.* 341–270 BCE) and his follower, the Roman Lucretius (*c.* 95–52 BCE). Thomas Nagel discusses this in his *Mortal Questions* (Cambridge: CUP, 1979). For more on being dead, at brief introductory level, see Peter Cave and Brendan Larvor, eds., *Thinking About Death* (London: British Humanist

Association, 2004). For a vastly deeper level, see Valberg (cited in Chapter 19's notes).

Chapter 21 Saints, sinners and suicide bombers

For the irrationality of not only religious belief but also some secular, see G. A. Cohen's work (notes to Chapter 22). On God's commands and morality, see Plato's dialogue on piety, namely, his *Euthyphro*, available in many Plato collections, for example, *The Last Days of Socrates* (London: Penguin Books, 1993).

The reference to all leaps being permitted is a quip on a comment associated with Dostoevsky's character Ivan Karamazov in *The Brothers Karamazov*. The thought that, if there is no God, everything is permitted is discussed by Jean-Paul Sartre (see Chapter 10's notes).

Chapter 22 A bit rich

This puzzle very much follows G. A. Cohen's *If You're an Egalitarian, How Come You're So Rich?* (Cambridge, Mass.; Harvard University Press, 2000). The book is an enjoyable read. Jerry – yes, curiously, 'Gerald' of the 'G' becomes an alphabetically advanced, albeit affectionate, 'J' – is not merely Oxford's Chichele Professor of Social and Political Theory but also something of a stand-up comic, having briefly trod Canadian boards when a teenager. Watch out for his impersonation of Isaiah Berlin.

Chapter 23 Uniquely who?

Having written this piece, I was then reminded by Ardon Lyon of Dostoevsky's *The Double*, based on meeting oneself. In the 1950s, such a story was submitted to *Granta* – by Lyon. It was rejected by the then editor, Michael Frayn.

On to serious stuff: some papers by Bernard Williams, reprinted in his *Problems of the Self* (Cambridge: CUP, 1973), are central to recent discussions. The fine and fertile work, responding to Williams and expanding the questions, is Derek Parfit's (see Chapter 6's notes). For a brief survey, see Ardon Lyon's 'Personal Identity', in G. H. R. Parkinson, ed., *An Encyclopaedia of Philosophy* (London: Routledge, 1988). An eccentric and intriguing approach, well worth reading, is found in Arnold Zuboff's 'One Self: The Logic of Experience', in the journal, *Inquiry*, 33 (London: Taylor & Francis, 1990). See also Zuboff and others in the collection, edited by Douglas R. Hofstadter and Daniel C. Dennett, *The Mind's I* (London: Penguin, 1982). For some most recent – and advanced – thoughts, try Valberg (cited in Chapter 19's notes). Franz Kafka's story is in *Metamorphosis and other stories*, trans. Willa and Edwin Muir (Harmondsworth: Penguin, 1961).

Chapter 24 Lucky for some

Moral luck was mischievously labelled thus by Bernard Williams in a 1976 paper, replied to by Thomas Nagel. Williams' paper is in his *Moral Luck* (Cambridge: CUP, 1981).

Nagel's appears in his *Mortal Questions* (see Chapter 20's notes). Nagel's collection is easier to handle than Williams'. The problem derives from Kant (see notes to Chapter 13). For the jewel shining, see Kant, *Groundwork of the Metaphysics of Morals*, trans. Mary Gregor (Cambridge: CUP, 1998), §1. For the vanishing 'I', see also Chappell (cited in Chapter 19's notes).

Chapter 25 'I shot the sheriff'

Clark ('Further reading') has labelled this the 'paradox of jurisdiction'. For discussion of actions, see G. E. M. Anscombe's *Intention* (Chapter 7's notes).

Chapter 26 You'll never get to heaven

Kant stresses the concern for motivation (Chapter 24's notes). Mill's thoughts on happiness and utilitarianism are in his *Utilitarianism* (many editions). I have raised a puzzle about motivation. A related puzzle is Pascal's Wager, which argues that it is prudent to believe in God; but the problem is how could that alone lead to belief? Would the motivation to believe distort the belief's sincerity?

Chapter 27 Chicken! Chicken! Chicken!

Prisoner's dilemmas abound. An accessible survey is William Poundstone, *Prisoner's Dilemma* (New York: Doubleday, 1992).

Chapter 28 Tensions in tense

Metaphysical problems of time do not generate easy readings (present entry excepted, of course). A good detailed collection is by Robin le Poidevin and Murray MacBeath, eds., *The Philosophy of Time* (Oxford: OUP, 1993). John McTaggart Ellis McTaggart (1866–1925) – what a splendid name! – offers in his two volume *The Nature of Existence* an idiosyncratic idealism (space and time both, in some way, being illusory), with reality consisting of loving souls. His 'unreality of time' argument is in Poidevin and MacBeath. Wittgenstein and poker have now reached book-length investigation. See David Edmonds and John Eidinow, *Wittgenstein's Poker* (London: Faber & Faber, 2001). For detailed, difficult, excellent and crisp work on time, try D. H. Mellor's *Real Time II* (London: Routledge, 1998).

Chapter 29 'I am a robot'

The question 'What is it like to be a bat?' was posed by Timothy Sprigge; but became much discussed through Nagel's paper in his *Mortal Questions* (see Chapter 20's notes). Good introductory works are Edward Feser's *Philosophy of Mind: A Beginner's Guide* (Oxford: Oneworld, 2005) and Keith Frankish's *Consciousness* (London: Routledge, 2005), with explanations of 'zombies' and, in the latter, even 'zimbies' (yes, it gets worse). There is also John Wisdom's *Other Minds*, 2nd ed. (Oxford: Basil Blackwell, 1965). Many consider it quaint and enigmatic – a few of us delight and admire.

Chapter 30 Eye spy

See Alfred Lessing, 'What is Wrong with a Forgery?' reprinted in Neill and Ridley (see note to Chapter 2). A biography of Blunt is by Miranda Carter, *Anthony Blunt: His Lives* (London: Macmillan, 2001), though a quick scan identified some small errors (it shows my age). A recent work on van Meegeren is Frank Wynne's *I Was Vermeer: The Legend of the Forger Who Swindled the Nazis* (London: Bloomsbury, 2006). For reference to Wittgenstein's poker, see Chapter 28's notes.

Chapter 31 Don't read this notice

Epimenides (sixth century BCE), a Cretan, famously said, 'The Cretans always lie.' If some other Cretan speaks truly, that will be simply false, but if not, then we have a paradox akin to 'I am lying'. The comment is in the New Testament, Epistle of Paul to Titus, 1:12, 'One of themselves, even a prophet of their own, said, "The Cretans are always liars, evil beasts, slow bellies."'

The Liar itself is usually credited to Eubulides, a fourth-century (BCE) logician from Megara. See Diogenes Laertius, *Lives of the Philosophers* II.108. Allegedly, Philetus of Cos worried so much about the Liar that he died. Plato reports Socrates as saying that philosophizing is practising dying. Well, Philetus seems a case where practising became perfect.

Chapter 32 Mysteries

See J. L. Mackie, *The Miracle of Theism* (Oxford: Clarendon Press, 1982). Recent intelligent design is discussed in Neil A. Manson, ed., *God and Design* (London: Routledge, 2003). For time existing without change, see Shoemaker's paper in *The Philosophy of Time* collection (details in Chapter 28).

Talk of many universes arguably derives from Leibniz's possible worlds: for this and his principle of sufficient reason, see the collection cited in Chapter 15. Most philosophers stress that such worlds are merely possible, lacking any existence akin to our actual world. Scientists, however, when speaking of many universes are speaking of universes that exist just as this one does, albeit inaccessibly so. David Lewis holds a view most akin to this latter. He argues that the only difference between possible universes and the actual universe is that the latter is *this* one. See his *On the Plurality of Worlds* (Oxford: Basil Blackwell, 1986).

Concerning something out of nothing, we may note Benjamin Disraeli's novel, *Tancred* (published 1847), where we find Lady Constance commenting on a scientific treatise in which, 'everything is explained by geology and astronomy and in that way . . . You know, all is development. The principle is perpetually going on. First, there was nothing, then there was something; then, I forget the next, I think there were shells, then fishes . . .' What should we make of that by way of explanation?

Chapter 33 Is this all there is?

The title refers to the Peggy Lee song 'Is That All There Is?' written by Jerry Leiber and Mike Stoller. The incidents in the song apparently derive from Thomas Mann's short story *Disillusionment*. That affection may animate inanimate objects is manifested in a recent loss, or transformation, of Silver Streak, a car that did her best for twenty years; she could not go on. Tennyson's poem, *Blow, Bugle, Blow*, forms part of Benjamin Britten's beautiful and disturbing *Serenade for tenor, horn and strings*.

Oswald Hanfling discusses life's meaning in his highly readable *The Quest for Meaning* (Oxford: Blackwell/Open University, 1987). A collection, including extracts from Schopenhauer, is Ossie's *Life and Meaning* (Oxford: Blackwell, 1987). For the tedium of immortality, see Bernard Williams, cited in notes to Chapter 23. Samuel Beckett's *Happy Days* (London: Faber and Faber, 2006) and many of his other works aid reflection on (and, intriguingly, sometimes enjoyment in) life's starkness and meaning – or lack thereof.

INDEX

References to entire chapters are in **bold**.

What's Wrong with Eating People?

- When is a gin and tonic not a gin and tonic?
- Why save endangered species?
- Should men and women be treated equally?
- When does "yes" mean "no"?
- Are we more than our brains?

Peter Cave's second volume of puzzling paradoxes, logical loopholes, and classic conundrums carves up life's most important questions with clarity, sparkle, and humour. Served with generous helpings of tall stories and quirky cartoons, *What's Wrong with Eating People?* boasts a menu ranging from logic to love, ethics to art. A feast of fun for all ages – especially those who loved the brilliantly successful *Can a Robot be Human?*

"Britain's wittiest philosopher on top form."
Raymond Tallis
Author of *The Kingdom of Infinite Space*

ISBN 978-1-85168-620-9 £7.99/$12.95

42

Drawing his inspiration from 42 of the funniest, wisest, and quirkiest quotations on the big questions in life, Vernon offers a light-hearted look at what philosophy has to say about life, the Universe, and everything. Deftly interweaving the thoughts of the greatest minds of all time, from Socrates to Monty Python, Vernon provides a platter of witty yet profound discussions on work, love, eternal life, sex, and happiness. From the allure of cats to the nature of wisdom, this rip-roaring read is the perfect companion for the armchair philosopher, and proves that even a little introspection can transform our lives for the better!

"A joy to read, yielding both wisdom and delight in perfectly sized portions."
Prof Richard Schoch, Queen Mary College, University of London

ISBN 978-1-85168-560-8 £9.99/$14.95

Why Don't Spiders Stick to their Webs?

- What would happen if you fell into a black hole?
- Which properties give you the best chance of winning at Monopoly?
- And why is it always so difficult to get ketchup to come out of a full bottle?

Award winning science writer Robert Matthews has provided answers to the most baffling, intriguing, and occasionally downright trivial questions received from members of the public, and has come up with some surprising results. From the farthest reaches of the universe to the mysterious fate of odd socks, this collection of questions and answers unravels the science behind the world around us, disproving once and for all the theory that science is just something that balding men in lab coats do to pass the time.

Robert Matthews is Visiting Reader in Science at Aston University, Birmingham, UK. He has published pioneering research in fields ranging from code-breaking to the probability of coincidences, and won an Ig Nobel Prize for his studies of Murphy's Law, including the reasons why toast so often lands butter-side down.

"A thrill-ride for curious minds"
John Rennie, editor-in-chief of *Scientific American*

ISBN 978-1-85168-551-6 £7.99/$14.95

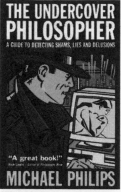
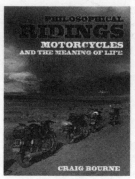